ARCHIVES

DICTIONARY
OF INDIANS
OF NORTH AMERICA

DICTIONARY
OF INDIANS
OF NORTH AMERICA

3

SCHOLARY PRESS, INC.
19722 EAST NINE MILE RD.
ST. CLAIR SHORES, MICHIGAN 48080

R

RAIN-IN-THE-FACE (Dakota; 1835–1905) was a noted Sioux warrior and chief. He was a full-blood Hunkpapa, one of a family of six brothers, one of whom was known as Iron Horse. Shortly before his death, he said: "My father was not a chief; my grandfather was not a chief, but a good hunter and a feast-maker. On my mother's side I had some noted ancestors, but they left me no chieftainship. I had to work for my reputation." He received his common name as the result of a personal encounter, when about 10 years of age, with a Cheyenne boy; he received several blows in the face causing it to be spattered with blood and streaked where the paint had been washed away. When a young man, he joined a war-party against the Gros Ventre, some of whose horses they stole, but the Sioux party was overtaken and had to fight for their lives. Rain-in-the-Face had his face painted to represent the sun when half covered with darkness—half black and half red. Fighting all day in the rain, his face became partly washed and streaked with red and black, so again he was named Rain-in-the-Face. He had been many times on the warpath, but his first important experience as a warrior was in the attack on the troops near Ft. Phil Kearny, Wyo., in Dec. 1866, in which Capt. Fetterman and his entire command of 80 men were killed. He participated also in a fight, two years later, near Ft. Totten, Dak., in which he and his horse were wounded. About three years before the Custer massacre in 1876, Rain-in-the-Face was accused of killing a surgeon and a trader of Gen. Stanley's expedition, for which he was arrested by Col. Thomas Custer. Having confessed his guilt, he was imprisoned for a time, but was allowed by his guard to escape and joined Sitting Bull's band of hostiles in the spring of 1874, declaring that he would "cut the heart out of Tom Custer and eat it." Rain-in-the-Face was a leading participant in the Little Bighorn fight, and although it has frequently been stated that he personally killed Gen. Custer, this is now generally doubted, and was denied by him. From wounds received in this battle he was permanently lamed, yet he followed Sitting Bull into Canada, where he remained until 1880, when most of the fugitives surrendered to Gen. Miles at Ft Keogh, Montana.

RANTCHEWAIME (Iowa) or *Female Flying Tiger*, was the wife of Mahaskah.

RAYMOND, ARTHUR (Dakota; 20th century), a journalist, became the first Sioux Indian to be elected to the North Dakota state legislature. Raymond was born in Winner, South Dakota, and educated at Dakota Wesleyan University. He began his career as a reporter on the *Mitchell Daily Republic* and later became Sunday editor of the *Grand Forks Herald*. In 1971 he was appointed director of Indian studies at the University of North Dakota.

RED BIRD (Winnebago; 1788—February 16, 1828), properly Wanigsuchka, was the Winnebago war chief who led the outbreak of 1827. The settlers at Prairie du Chien, Wisconsin long considered Red Bird their friend and protector. In 1827 two Winnebago Indians were arrested for the murder of a white family. A false rumor that the two had been surrendered to the Chippewa, traditional enemies of the Winnebago, and had been killed while running the gauntlet reached the Winnebago chiefs. Whether this indeed was the reason for the outbreak is not entirely clear, but the chiefs did convene a council which chose Red Bird to seek revenge.

On June 26, 1827, he and two warriors proceeded to Prairie du Chien where they killed the registrar and his servant. They then joined 37 other warriors with their families at the mouth of the Bad Axe River in Minnesota. On the 27th or 28th the band attacked two keel boats on the Mississippi River and killed four crewmen. When the boats reached

Galena, Illinois, a force of mounted volunteers was organized with Henry Dodge as captain, and, when word of the outbreak reached the garrison at St. Louis, Missouri, 500 regular troops were dispatched under Gen. Henry Atkinson to attack the Winnebago. Atkinson and Dodge pursued Red Bird up the Wisconsin River while another force of regulars dispatched from Fort Howard (Greenbay, Wisconsin) under Maj. William Whistler proceeded up the Fox River. Finding himself vastly outnumbered by an incredible overreaction of the settlers and trapped between two advancing forces, Red Bird surrendered. He was tried, convicted and transported to Fort Crawford (Prairie du Chien) where he died on February 16, 1828 still awaiting sentencing.

RED CLOUD (Oglala Sioux; 1822–1909), was a principal chief of the Oglala Teton Sioux of Pine Ridge Reservation, the largest band of the Sioux nation, and probably the most famous and powerful chief in the history of the tribe. The origin of the name is disputed, but is said to refer to the way in which his scarlet-blanketed warriors formerly covered the hillsides like a red cloud. If this is true, the name was bestowed after he had obtained recognition as a leader.

Red Cloud was born at the forks of Platte River, Nebraska, and died at Pine Ridge, South Dakota. He was a member of the Snake family, the most distinguished and forceful of his tribe, and rose to prominence by his own force of character, having no claim to hereditary chiefship, which in the Oglala band rested with the family represented by They-fear-even-his-horse ("Young-man-afraid-of-his-horses") and more friendly toward civilization. When in 1865 the Government undertook to build a road from Ft. Laramie, Wyoming, on the North Platte, by way of Powder River, to the gold regions of Montana, Red Cloud headed the opposition for his tribe, on the ground that the influx of travel along the trail would destroy the best remaining buffalo ground of the Indians. The first small detachment of troops sent out to begin construction work were intercepted by Red Cloud with a large party of Oglala Sioux and Cheyenne, and held practically as prisoners for more than two weeks, but finally were allowed to proceed when it seemed to the chief that they might be massacred by his young men. In the fall of the same year commissioners were sent to treat with the Oglala for permission to build the road, but Red Cloud forbade the negotiations.

On June 30, 1866, another council for the same purpose was called at Ft Laramie, Red Cloud this time attending and repeating his refusal to endanger the hunting grounds of his people. While he was speaking, a strong force of troops under Gen. Carrington arrived, and on being told, in reply to a question, that they had come to build forts and open the road to Montana, he seized his rifle and with a final defiant message left the council with his entire following. Carrington then set out on his mission, which included the rebuilding and garrisoning of Ft. Reno, on Powder River, and the establishment of Ft. Phil Kearny and Ft. C.F. Smith, the last named was on Bighorn River, in Montana. Another protest to Carrington himself proving ineffectual, Red Cloud surrounded the troops and working force at Ft. Kearny with perhaps 2,000 warriors and harassed them so constantly that not even a load of hay could be brought in from the prairie except under the protection of a strong guard, while it was made impossible to venture out after the game that was abundant all around. On December 21, 1866, an entire detachment of 81 men under Capt. Fetterman was cut off and every man killed. On August 1, 1867, another severe engagement occurred near the post. In all this time not a single wagon had been able to pass over the road, and in 1868 another commission was appointed to come to terms with Red Cloud, who demanded as an ultimatum the abandonment of the three posts and of all further attempts to open the Montana road. A treaty was finally made on this basis, defining the limits of the Sioux country as claimed by the Sioux, Red Cloud refusing to sign or even to be present until the garrisons had actually been withdrawn, thus winning a complete victory for the position which he had taken from the beginning. He finally affixed his signature at Ft Laramie, Nov. 6, 1868. From that date he seems to have kept his promise to live at peace with the whites, although constantly resisting the innovations of civilization. He took no active part in the Sioux war of 1876, although he is accused of having secretly aided and encouraged the hostiles. Convinced of the hoplessness of attempting to hold the Black Hills after the discovery of gold in that region, he joined in the agreement of cession in 1876. In the outbreak of 1890-91 he also remained quiet, then an old man and partially blind, and was even said to have been threatened by the hostiles on account of his loyal attitude toward the Government.

As a warrior Red Cloud stood first among his people, having counted 80 coups or separate deeds of bravery in battle. As a general and statesman he ranked equally high, having been long prominent in treaties and councils, and several times a delegate to Washington, his attitude always that of a patriot from the Indian standpoint. Personally he was described by one well acquainted with him as a most courtly chief and a natural-born gentleman, with a bow as graceful as that of a Chesterfield. For some years before his death he was blind and lived in a house built for him by the Government.

RED FISH (Yanktonai) was also called *Hogan Luta.*

RED JACKET (Seneca; *c.* 1758– January 20, 1830), though accused of cowardice in battle, used his gift for oratory to maintain his position as chief of the Senecas. Red Jacket, of course, was his English name, bestowed upon him as a result of the succession of red coats he wore while on the British side during the American Revolution. His first Indian name was Otetiani, but he assummed the name Sagoyewatha upon his election to the Seneca chieftainship.

The Seneca—as did most of the Iroquois League tribes—sided with the British during the Revolution. Red Jacket, along with some Seneca warriors, though, retreated precipitously at the approach of General Sullivan's troops in 1779. He even attempted to conclude a separate peace with the Americans, but his plans were frustrated by Mohawk chief Joseph Brant. For all of these actions, Red Jacket was considered a coward by many of his own people. When many of the braver chiefs and warriors were killed, moreover, Red Jacket seized the opportunity to consolidate his power. In 1786, at an Indian council along the Detroit River, Red Jacket put his splendid oratorical skills to protesting the inevitable peacemaking with the United States; most likely, the hostile position he assumed was political trickery aimed primarily at currying favor with those who had thought their chief cowardly in combat.

Red Jacket constantly sought to portray himself as a bitter enemy of the whites and protector of his people, but to a great extent his oratory was a facade, masking his naked ambition for all forms of self aggrandizement. For example, in 1787, 1788, and 1790, he publicly opposed land sales in order to maintain his popularity with the Seneca, but he secretly signed the property cessions in order to protect his prestige with the Americans. As he strengthened his leadership position, however, he seems to have become more sincere in his protestations against white influence upon the customs, religion, and language of his tribe.

Red Jacket vehemently opposed missionaries living on Indian lands. Following the New York legislature's decree forbidding white residence on Indian territory (1821), Red Jacket led a contingent of the tribe in ousting the local missionary. He also attempted—but this time in vain—to preserve Indian jurisdiction over criminal acts committed on Indian property. In the Tommy Jemmy case (1821), Red Jacket stated that the Seneca council which had tried a squaw for witchcraft and the warrior who had executed her were outside the jurisdiction of the United States.

During the 1820s, Red Jacket began to lose prestige as his drinking and general dissipation grew more observable. In 1827 his wife joined the church, and Red Jacket fulfilled his threat to leave her, an action which prompted his further degeneration. Although he returned to his wife a few months later, he was deposed as chief by a council of 26 tribal leaders—only to be reinstated through a personal effort at reform and the help of the U.S. Office of Indian Affairs.

The reinstated chief quickly fell back into his old ways, however. By the time of his death in 1830, Red Jacket's anti-white and anti-Christian policies were long out of date, and he was surrounded by a largely Christianized tribe in which he was an alien presence. In fact—though his wishes were to the contrary—Red Jacket was given a Christian funeral and was buried in the cemetary of his reservation's Christian mission.

RED TOMAHAWK (Dakota) or *Ospecannonpa*, born in 1853 was the Indian policeman who shot Sitting Bull.

REIFEL, BEN (Dakota; 20th century), a Rosebud Sioux Indian, is one of the most distinguished of contemporary Indian leaders.

Born on the Rosebud reservation in South Dakota, Reifel grew up in that bleak country on the small farm owned by his father.

His mother was a full blood Sioux from one of the leading families. His father was a German who had worked for the Indian Agency and with marriage into the tribe, received some land for a small homestead. Altogether, there were four sons.

From the time he was a small boy, Ben had trudged over the land, helping with the planting and growing of the few crops that could be raised. As he grew older, he helped with the care of the cattle and horses. He grew accustomed to hard backbreaking labor, with little time for play, but he wondered if there wasn't a way to make things grow better and to make work easier.

In spite of his youth, he reasoned that the Indian people lived too much in the past and that attitudes would have to change. He was drawn to the larger world outside the reservation, longing to be, and determined to be, a part of it.

His mother encouraged Ben in his yearnings. She said that he must make something of himself, that he must go to school and become a credit to his people. But his harder-headed father scoffed at this. Ben was to be a farmer and schooling wasn't necessary.

So Ben worked on the farm, going to school only when the work wasn't heavy and when he could get away. He didn't complete 8th grade work until he was 16 because of this interrupted attendance, but his plans to go to high school were shattered when his father put his foot down. There was to be no more schooling

Ben remained on the farm for three years, stifling the desire for an education as best he could. Like others who found inspiration in stories of the great men of history, Ben read over and over a collection of biographies that had somehow come into his possession. Books were few and far between on the isolated farm. He drew strength from these stories and from them came the courage to run away from home — 250 miles away to enroll in high school.

His father, perhaps understanding at last that his son was not to be swayed from his determination, made no effort to make him return home.

In high school, Ben was a student of exceptional ability. Friends decided that he must go on to college and they helped him to accomplish this. Because of his farming background, and motiviated by an interest in improving farm conditions, he majored in chemistry and dairy science.

When he eventually obtained his master's degree, he was appointed farm agent on the Pine Ridge reservation by the Bureau of Indian Affairs. He enjoyed working with his people, helping them to get greater yields from their poor acres.

While Ben was in college he was commissioned a Second Lieutenant in the U.S. Army Reserves. He also met the young woman whom he married.

With the outbreak of World War II, he was ordered to active duty and after serving to the War's end, was returned to inactive status as a Lt. Colonel. He was also appointed superintendent on the Fort Berthold Agency in North Dakota.

The zeal for an education still burned, so he accepted a scholarship to Harvard and obtained his master's in public administration. On another scholarship at the same institution, he completed studies for his doctorate. He was one of the first American Indians to receive the Ph.D.

His next assignment with the Bureau of Indian Affairs was that of organization field agent, helping tribes form business structures under the provisions of the Indian Reorganization Act of 1932. He then became superintendent of Pine Ridge Agency, the first Indian superintendent of that reservation, and one of the first of Indian blood to be an agency superintendent in the Indian Service. His fine record rapidly opened the doors for others as they became qualified.

Ben always spoke forthrightly to his people. He expressed to them his philosophy that habits and thought patterns that were negative and prevented progress must be changed. He assured them that he was always on their side and willing to help them.

"It is we who must be aware of what our problems are, he said. It is we who must search for answers and we who must evolve plans that will be ours and for which we are willing to fight, struggle and sacrifice. We must adapt ourselves as our forefathers did and turn our backs on what is gone and of no more use."

His mother had instilled this thinking in him, telling him that there must be a proper blending of old and new, a discarding of weaknesses and a holding on to strengths.

This was a courageous position to take in a situation where traditionalism was well entrenched. It did not make his work easy but it won him respect for having the courage of his convictions.

Before he left the Indian Service for good, Reifel was appointed Area Director for the Bureau of Indian Affairs in Aberdeen, South Dakota. He was responsible for the functioning of the large number of Indian agencies and schools in the two Dakotas and Nebraska.

But again, a larger world beckoned. He resigned from the Aberdeen office in 1960 to run as Republican Congressman from South Dakota to the U.S. Congress. He easily defeated two well-known opponents in the primary and won a good pluraility in the elections. He remained in Congress for five terms, each time re-elected by larger margins, and his district was not a predominantly Indian one.

Reifel voluntarily retired from Congress in 1970, planning that he and Mrs. Reifel would travel extensively and enjoy their days together. He was asked to serve as a special consultant for Indian programs to the National Park Service and President Nixon appointed him chairman of the National Capitol Planning Commission, an agency acting both for the city of Washington and for the government in planning and reviewing all major construction projects in the District of Columbia.

Within a short time after his retirement, Mrs. Reifel (the former Alice Johnson, by whom he has one daughter, Loyce Reifel Anderson died very suddenly. Reifel is now married to a lifelong friend from college days. She is the former Frances Ryland Colby.

In 1960, Reifel was awarded the Indian Achievement Award, a national recognition presented by Indian Council Fire Achievement Award, Inc. On his retirement from Congress in 1970, he was awarded an honorary Doctor of Humanities degree by the University of South Dakota.

RENVILLE, GABRIEL (Sisseton).

RENVILLE JOSEPH (Dakota; 1779–1846), the half-Sioux son of a French fur-trader, was born in what is now St. Paul, Minnesota. Learning French at the age of 10 from a Catholic Priest, he became by the time he was 26 (1805) a guide to Lieutenant Z.M. Pike. He entered the service of the British in the War of 1812 as interpreter to the Sioux, with the rank of captain. He was present at Ft. Meigs and Ft. Stephenson, Ohio, and the good conduct of the Indians there was due largely to his influence. He went to the great council at Portage des Sioux (mouth of the Missouri) in 1815 as interpreter, and resigned his British commission and half pay to attach himself to the American interest. He organized the Columbia Fur Co., with headquarters on Lake Traverse, Minn., and, was able to meet the American Fur Co. on its own ground with strong competition. At the time of the consolidation Renville established an independent business at Lac qui Parle which he conducted until his death. In 1834 he met Dr. T. S. Williamson, the famous missionary, at Prairie du Chien, out on his first reconnoissance, and arranged with him to go to Lac qui Parle and establish a mission the next year. Williamson returned to Ohio for his family, and the next spring met Renville at Ft. Snelling, proceed to Lac qui Parle, which became the scene of most of his long service with the Sioux. They were soon joined by Dr.

S.R. Riggs, and engaged, with Renville's assistance, in the translation of the Scriptures. Renville translated every word of the Bible into the Dakota language, and the missionaries faithfully recorded it; he also rendered them invaluable assistance in the construction of the grammar and dictionary of the Dakota language. In 1841 Renville was chosen and ordained a ruling elder, discharging the duties of his office until his death at Lac qui Parle in Mar. 1846. Descendants still reside among the Sisseton Sioux in South Dakota.

REVENGER (Dakota) was a chief.

REYNOLDS, ALLIE P. (Creek; 20th century) was an outstanding pitcher for the New York Yankees in the 1940s.

RHOADES, EVERETT B. (Kiowa; October 24, 1931–   ), was the first Kiowa to earn a doctorate in medicine. He was born in Lawton, Oklahoma. Rhoades took his medical training at the University of Oklahoma and later became Chief of Infectious Diseases at the Veterans Administration Hospital at the university's medical center. He also served as a member of the Kiowa Tribal Council.

RICHARDSON, WILLIAM ROBERT (Haliwa; April 23, 1915–   ), was reared on a farm in a rural community. He attended public elementary school, and later furthered his education through a vocational training school, and home correspondence to high school equivalence. He enjoyed the leading roles in activities.

In the early thirties he took his first job cutting wood with an ax and mall, and stacking three cords per day. He saved to pay his fare to Philadelphia.

During World War II he joined the Civil Defense Service at the navy yard, and was rated as a first class machinist.

In 1953 he returned to Hollister, North Carolina in Halifax county to work with and for his people. He was elected as Chief of the Haliwa Indians, and still holds that position.

Under his leadership, the Haliwa Indians have made great progress. One of the achievements was an Indian School for the Indian children, with grades one through twelve being taught.

He helped to get this group of people recognized as the Haliwa Indian Tribe, the third largest tribe in North Carolina of about three thousand, located in Halifax and Warren counties. He drew up a court order for the purpose of getting any records pertaining to the Haliwa Indians that were incorrect, corrected.

He was founder and president of the Haliwa Mutual Burial Assn. In April 1972 he organized the first North Carolina Indian Commission in Raleigh, North Carolina and is chairman of that commission. In December 1972, he helped organize and name (CENA) Coalition Early Native Americans, Washington, D.C. which represented the Indians east of the Mississippi River. He has served as historian for the Haliwa Indians for sixteen years and is a member of the newly organized (NACDAC) Native American Curriculum Development Advisory Council.

In 1973 he took the initiative lead in getting Governor James Holshouser to attend the annual Haliwa Indian Pow-Wow, the first Governor to visit the festival. His Indian name is (Talking Eagle).

RICKLEFS, ELSIE GARDENER (Hoopa; February 2, 1920–   ), became the first woman chairman of the Hoopa Tribal Council. She was born in Korbel, California. Mrs. Ricklefs taught school for six years, helped orgainze a tribal credit union, and arranged programs on Hoopa culture for groups and schools. She was elected a regional vice-president of the National Congress of American Indians.

RIDDLE, TOBY (Modoc; 1843–?), or "Winema" was a Modoc woman who, together with her white husband, acted as chief interpretor in negotiations prior to and during the Modoc War of the 1870s. Personally of the opinion that any armed hostilities or resistance would be futile and fatal for her people, she consistently reported Modoc strategies to leaders of the American forces. Though her admonitions were ignored, her courage and integrity won her the respect of both sides and gained for her the title, *Pocahantas of the West* in the popular press and theatre of her day.

Toby Riddle was born about 1843 in a village at the upper end of the Link River in South Central Oregon. She was the daughter of Kintpuash's brother, Se-cot. Early in life she was called *The Strange Child* because she showed no fear of places held sacred by the tribe, and as an adult her bravery earned her the name *Little Woman Chief.* In 1861 she married Frank Riddle, a Kentucky-born rancher, ex-miner and hunter, and two years later she bore a son, Jeff (Chaka).

She is credited in 1869 with diffusing a potentially explosive situation arising at a peace conference between Kintpuash and A.B. Meacham, new Superintendant of Indian Affairs for Oregon.

Her conciliatory attempts were less successful four years later when, convinced that an assembled army intended to exterminate them, some Modocs formulated a plan to diffuse the attack by assasinating the enemy's leaders. Apprised of this strategy by a Modoc warrior named Weium, Toby warned General Canby and his party to at all costs avoid the conference arranged for Good Friday, April 11, 1874. However, she was unable to persuade the Americans of the danger she knew to be imminent; convinced that the Modocs *wouldn't dare*, they dismissed Toby as simply a foolish woman.

She confessed to the Modoc camp that she had betrayed their plan, but abolutely refused to name her informant. Her courage and sincerity won her the respect and protection of Kintpuash and other leaders, and she and her husband were spared when others in the negotiating party were assasinated as planned.

After the defeat of the Modocs and only a month after the execution of Kintpuash, the American public clamored for first hand accounts of the *Indian War*. To oblige, Meacham left his Indian Affairs post to organize a Modoc travelling show which toured Midwestern and Eastern cities. Toby Riddle was recruited as an attraction for this venture; she was billed as "Wi-ne-ma", a name reportedly lifted out of the romantic poetry of Joaquim Miller. Nothing further is known of her life.

RIDGE, JOHN (Cherokee; 1803 – June 22, 1839) or Skah-tle-loh-skee, the son of Major Ridge and successor of his father as chief of the Ridge faction among the Cherokees at the time of their removal westward, was born in Oothcaloga, Georgia, in 1803. Sharp and intelligent, he was sent to the mission school of the Moravian Brethren at Spring Place, Georgia, where he was given the beginning of an education in English. He followed his stay at Spring Place with a shorter stint at the Brainerd School conducted by missionaries sent to Cherokees by the American Board of Commissioners for Foreign Missions, and as a result of his record there he was selected by Elias Cornelius for attendance at the Foreign Mission School at Cornwall, Connecticut. There he finished his education, though not the course, impeded as he was by a severe case of scrofula of the hip. While there he fell in love with Sarah Bird Northrup, daughter of the steward of the school. Her parents, alarmed at the crippled condition of John's hip, agreed that if he went home and regained his health, they would consider the marriage of their daughter to him, in spite of public resentment toward the interracial match. He returned to Georgia and indeed recovered his health and presented himself in Corwall in early 1824 for the hand of Sarah Northrup. Near the same time his cousin Elias Boudinot sued for the hand of another Cornwall girl, Harriet Gold, an event which caused an even greater scandal, and the two cross-blood marriages played a strong role in the eventual closing of the Foreign Mission School.

On returning home John Ridge entered Cherokee politics for which he had been meticulously groomed. He also succeeded his father as ambassador to the Creeks and sat as a chief in their councils. In 1825 he went, with another Cherokee, David Vann, to Washington as secretary to the Creek delegation. Under Ridge's guidance the Creeks were able to abrogate the MacIntosh Treaty and save much of the Creeks' lands from the Federal government's maw. For this accomplishment John Ridge and Vann, as well as Major Ridge for his part in getting the negotiations under way, were rewarded with sizable stipends. Commissioner of Indian Affairs Thomas L. McKenny later managed to have Ridge broken as a Creek Chief. John Ridge then returned to Cherokee politics and was elected President of the National Committee, one of the highest elective positions in Cherokee government.

Like his father, staunchly anti-removal at first, he opposed all Federal government efforts to secure a treaty of removal. But he also came to see that there was no alternative to the Cherokees being destroyed as a nation if they remained in their ancestral lands—as had his father and his cousin Elias Boudinot, editor of the *Cherokee Phoenix* — and became a fervent supporter of removal. When the Treaty of New Echota was signed on December 29, 1835, by a small number of Treaty men, John Ridge had gone on to Washington to work out a pragmatic compromise between the Ross and the Treaty forces, but his effort failed, and he later signed the document in Washington.

Ridge became President of the Cherokee Committee for adjusting claims of emigrating Cherokees with the appropriate U.S. Commissioners. Many

Cherokees emigrating voluntarily took advantage of this arrangement, but not most of the much larger Ross faction. Late in 1837, with most of the Committee's business finished, John Ridge, his family, and Boudinot moved to their new home in the West. Ridge settled on Honey Creek, where he opened a store in partnership with his father. But the forced removal of the Ross faction in 1838 led to such bitter resentments that the Ridges and Boudinot, blamed for the plight of the Cherokees by the Ross faction, were murdered—or executed according to their enemies—at widely separated places on June 22, 1839.

RIDGE, JOHN ROLLIN (Cherokee; 1827– *c.* 1867), or Yellow Bird (Cheesquatalawny), the son of John Ridge and grandson of Major Ridge, was born at Ridge's Ferry (now Rome) Georgia. He went to California in 1850, became a leading journalist, wrote *Joaquin Murieta* (1854) and peoms published posthumously (1868), after his death in 1867.

RIDGE, MAJOR (Cherokee; *c.* 1771 –June 22, 1839, called Ka-nung-da-cla-geh, was a war chief of the Cherokees, born at Hiwassee, now Polk county, Tennessee, probably in 1771. His father taught the boy to hunt; in youth and young manhood he fought as a warrior in the border warfare between the whites and the Indians. After the establishment of peace he became a chief in the Cherokee council, where he distinguished himself as an orator and sponsor of liberal legislation. In the 1790s he settled with his wife, the former Susanna Wickett, on a farm in the Oothcaloga Valley, Georgia, and became an enthusiastic proponent of white civilization for the Cherokees.

When the War of 1812 broke out, Ridge suppored the American cause in council and later helped organize Cherokee volunteers to fight under Andrew Jackson against the Creeks. He distinguished himself in the Creek War and took his highest rank,

Major, as his first name. A leading advocate of white education, he sent his children to schools run by missionaries of the Morvian Brethren and of the American Board of Commissioners for Foreign Missions, such as the Foreign Mission School at Cornwall, Connecticut, attended by his son John.

Major Ridge rose to the top echelon of men governing the Cherokee Nation. In 1827, after the death of Chiefs Pathkiller and Charles Hicks, the executive government devolved on him as Speaker of the Council, and on John Ross as President of the National Committee. When John Ross was elected Principal Chief, Major Ridge was elevated to the new post of Counselor which he retained until he was dismissed for his later pro-removal stand. For years he had been adamant against moving the Nation beyond the Mississippi from their ancestral lands in southern Appalachia—years when he flourished as a slave-owning master of a fine plantation at Ridge's Ferry on the Oostanaula River in Georgia, and as a partner in a thriving trading post there, becoming one of the richest men in the Cherokee Nation. But as Cherokee affairs worsened under Georgia's discriminatory laws and under the onslaughts of Georgia whites who wanted the Cherokee lands, he joined his son John and his nephew Elias Boudinot in advocating removal. As he became the leader of the Treaty or Removal Party, opposed to the delaying policy of John Ross's faction, his popularity waned, and dissension was tearing the Nation apart. The Ridge faction saw resistance to the white pressures for removal as hopeless and leading to disaster. They demanded that drastic steps be taken to effect a removal treaty which would buy the Cherokees time, in their new lands in the West, the present Oklahoma, to educate themselves for more effective competition with the white man.

Under Major Ridge's leadership, the Treaty of New Echota was signed on December 29, 1835, by men representing only a minority of the tribe. But it was ratified by the U.S. Senate, providing for removal westward, for the exchange of land and for certain funds that guaranteed among other things the education of Cherokee youth. The majority, led by John Ross, refused to accept the Treaty as the will of the Nation, failed to prepare for the removal and, unlike most of the Treaty advocates, were in 1838 brutally driven from the land of their birth. Such were the hardships of the trek, the notorious Trail of Tears, that many thousands died on the way. The resulting hatred against the Ridges and Boudinot as leading advocates of removal was such that an unauthorized execution party, invoking the ancient Cherokee Blood Law, murdered Major Ridge, John Ridge, and Elias Boudinot on June 22, 1839, at widely different localities. Major Ridge fell on the Line Road just inside Arkansas. The Ross-Ridge feud that followed bred dissension in the Nation until after the Civil War.

ROBERT I (Mosquito; fl. 18th century), Robert Charles Frederick, succeeded his brother George III in 1825 as Britain's puppet on Nicaragua's Mosquito Coast. A particularly incompetent ruler, Robert yielded his limited powers to the English superintendent of Belize (British Honduras), Alexander MacDonald. His son George IV took the throne in 1841, a year before Robert died.

ROBERT II (Mosquito; 1876–1908), Robert Henry Clarence, called Chief Clarence, was the last Mosquito Indian king of Nicaragua's British-controlled Mosquito Coast. Born in 1876, he succeeded his cousin Jonathan I in 1890. Nicaragua's government ousted him in 1894, his territory becoming Zelaya department. Robert retired to Jamaica, where he died in 1908.

ROBINSON, ALEXANDER (Potawatomi; 1789– ?), a Potawatomi chief also called Cheecheebingway, firmly opposed the needless kill-

ing of whites. Born in Mackinaw, Michigan to a
Scotish trader and an Ottawa woman, Robinson
participated in the surrender of Fort Dearborn during the War of 1812. Under Captain Nathaniel
Heald the fort had maintained friendly relations
with the Winnebago and Potawatomi, but not
friendly enough to counter British influence. When
Heald was ordered to retreat to Fort Wayne, the 500
Potawatomi he mistakenly asked to escort him
attacked his group of 91 soldiers with families.
Robinson, trying but failing to prevent the massacre of the whites, managed to save Heald and his
wife (2 of 27 who survived).

In 1820 Robinson acted as an interpreter for Gen.
Lewis Cass in negotiating a treaty with the Chippewa (June 6), and in 1827 restrained his younger
warriors from again attacking Fort Dearborn. Signing the July 7, 1829 Treaty of Prairie du Chien,
Wisconsin, which delineated boundaries among the
"Northwest" tribes, Robinson supported the white
settlers during the Black Hawk War of 1832, and
joined the forces of Gen. Henry Atkinson in pursuit
of Black Hawk.

ROBINSON, CHARLIE (San Blas; fl. 1920 and
1930s), was a San Blas Indian leader of Panama
who during the 1920s and 1930s allied with chiefs
Nele de Cantule and Ina Paquina to stage an independence movement (1925) and a violent protest
during the controversial national election of 1932.
When the Panamanian government in 1930 re-
formed laws regarding Indian reservations, Charlie
Robinson attempted to regain for the Indians two of
their villages.

ROCK, HOWARD (Iniut; 1910–   ), became
Editor of the *Tundra Times*, a weekly newspaper
published at Fairbanks, Alaska. Under Rock's leadership, the *Times* flourished as a "crusading" publication.

Rock was born on August 10, 1911 in Point Hope,

Alaska. He attended St. Thomas Mission School and various schools in Alaska. In his twenties, Rock worked his passage to the Northwest area of the United States. In Oregon he studied art with a private teacher; later he studied art formally at the University of Washington.

After completing his studies, he designed jewelry and craft items embodying Eskimo motifs. After a short time at this work, Rock was drafted into military service. He served in the U. S. army air corps from 1943 to 1945, in North Africa.

After his military service, Rock returned to the area of jewelry design. In the 1950s, he decided to return to Point Hope and to concentrate his energies on painting.

Becoming involved in community meetings in Point Hope, Rock began to turn his attention to the need for an effective form of communication among the Eskimo people in the area. Rock found support among Eskimo leaders for the idea of a publication controlled by the "Natives." Eventually, Rock secured a financial backer and began putting out the *Tundra Times* in 1962.

Though Rock had no formal journalistic training or experience, he was strongly motivated to make a success of the *Times*. He secured experienced journalists for his staff and was a "quick study" as Editor. As a matter of basic policy, Rock took strong editorial stands whenever he felt them appropriate or necessary. Rock and the *Times*, for example, have been praised, for their efforts to publicize the problems of the Pribilof Islanders.

Rock's acclaimed efforts on the *Tundra Times* must be seen as part of the total movement toward self-determination and self-expression among North American Indians in the 1960s.

ROGERS, WILL (Cherokee; November 4, 1879– August 15, 1935), a Cherokee Indian, was a humorist, actor, and columnist in the early 20th century. He achieved a nationwide reputation, and widespread affection, for his achievements as a performer and a homespun philosopher. It was only in the 1960s, however, long after his death, that attention was directed to him as an Indian and as an Indian spokesman.

Rogers was born at Ololgah, Indian Territory (later the state of Oklahoma). He received little formal education and began his career as a cowboy in wild west shows and the like.

His long career in vaudeville began in 1905. Will Rogers appeared in a Florence Ziegfield show for the first time in 1914, the start of a long association with Ziegfield. As early as 1915, he began putting political material into his humor routines.

Rogers developed a newspaper column based mainly on his political commentary. His column was syndicated on a weekly basis in 1922, then daily in 1926.

In his writing Rogers made abundant use of homely metaphors and, occasionally, country dialects. This writing style seemed actually to enchance the sharp incisive nature of his comments.

Will Rogers was particularly sharp on the subject of ralations between the U. S. government and the American Indian. He often developed the theme that in most wars, particularly the Indian wars, noble slogans served only to mask the main objective: acquisition of land.

In the course of his varied career, Rogers also worked as a motion picture actor for three years. He appeared in films such as *A Connecticut Yankee* (1931) and *State Fair* (1933). He died along with pilot Wiley Post in a plane crash in Alaska on August 15, 1935.

A popular thinker who used humor to convey his social and political ideas, Rogers wrote a number of books. These included *The Cowboy Philosopher on Prohibition* (1919), *What We Laugh At* (1920), *Illiterate Digest* (1924), and *There's Not a Bathing Suit in Russia* (1927).

ROLFE, THOMAS (Powhatan; 1617—?   ), was the only child of Pocahontas and John Rolfe. Born in 1617 (shortly before Pocahontas died) in England, rolfe was educated in London; but he returned to Virginia around 1641 and attempted to visit his mother's tribe—then at war with the colonists. Little else regarding Thomas Rolfe's life was recorded.

ROMAN NOSE (Cheyenne; fl. 19th century), although not a chief, is remembered not only for his influence and leadership, but also for his seeming invulnerability in battle.

A medicine man named Ice made a protective war bonnet for Roman Nose. Both his followers and his enemies had reason to respect that magnificient headpiece, for time after time they had seen him—an imposing 6'3" figure mounted on a splendid horse—ride close to the enemy at a leisurely pace. Bullets and arrows simply passed him by. This display quite naturally inspired his companions to brave deeds.

There were certain taboos connected with the bonnet. If the wearer did not observe them, the magic vanished. For example, Roman Nose could not eat food that had been removed from a pot or dish with an iron instrument. His food must be removed with a forked stick. The curse could be ended, but only by long, elaborate purification rites.

Between 1864 and 1868 Roman Nose was prominent in fights along the Kansas frontier, attacking gangs laying rails for what he called noisy wagons (steam engines for the Kansas Pacific Railroad), killing settlers, running off livestock, burning and sacking.

To put an end to these depradations, Major George A. Forsyth asked for and received permission to raise a body of scouts—50 hardy frontiersmen. His second in command was Lt. Fred Beecher. They tracked the Cheyennes northward from Fort Hayes to their camp on the Arickaree

Fork of the Republian River, where Beecher Island is located. The eight-day fight began on September 17, and before sundown Roman Nose was dead, just as he had predicted he would be when he learned that he had broken one of the laws that came with his bonnet. The guest of a Sioux family the night before, he did not notice when the woman used a metal fork to lift some bread from a pan. When someone called his attention to the misdeed, he said, "That breaks my medicine." He would have gone through the purification ceremony, as urged to do so by Tall Bull, but there was no time after the scouts were sighted. Roman Nose rode into battle and was almost immediately shot in the back. Friends managed to get him to the Indian camp, where he died.

ROSS, JOHN (Cherokee; October 3, 1790– August 1, 1866), was a principal chief of the Cherokees from 1828–1866. It was during this time the Cherokees were forced from their ancestral homes in Alabama, Georgia, North Carolina, and Tennessee. The migration was to become known as The Trail of Tears. Ross became the leader of the National Party of the Cherokees. This group wanted to remain on their ancestral homelands and were in opposition to John Ridge and his Treaty Party. The Treaty Party advocated voluntary Cherokee removal and payment for ceded lands.

Ross was born in Rossville, Geogia. He was the son of Daniel Ross, a native of Scotland, and Mollie McDonald, who was only ¼ Cherokee descent. His maternal grandfather was John McDonald, who was a native of Scotland and the tory agent among the Chickamaugau during the American Revolution. Ross was ⅛ Cherokee. He had blue eyes and brown hair. He could easily pass for a white man. John Ross was a Methodist and was educated at an Academy at Kingsport, Tennessee.

John Ross's claim to prominence among the Cherokee was not hereditary, since his clan designation seems to be unknown. He was chosen for his first effort among the Cherokee by the white Indian agent. Ross was sent to contact the Cherokee in Arkansas in 1809.

Ross' second step to prominence was when he was adjutant of the Cherokee forces against the Creeks in 1813-14. This Cherokee regiment served under General Andrew Jackson against the Creek faction known as Red Sticks. Little did Ross know· then, that General Jackson was going to be the foe of the Cherokee just as he was now the foe of the "Red Sticks" who didn't want to give up their land to white settlers.

John Ross was elected to fill the office of principal chief in 1828, one month before the traditional enemy of the Cherokee, Andrew Jackson, was elected President of the United States. Ross' troubles were in clear focus when President Andrew Jackson succeeded in getting the Indian Removal Bill passed. From that time till the Trail of Tears march to Indian Territory, John Ross worked for non-removal.

All was not in agreement in the Cherokee Nation. Many felt that a removal treaty advantageous to the Cherokees should be negotiated with President Andrew Jackson. This faction within the Cherokee Nation was being led by John Ridge and Elias Boudinot. Therefore, John Ross was not at New Echota on December 29, 1835, when the pro-treaty faction, led by John Ridge, signed the removal treaty in which the Cherokee nation ceded and relinquished title to all lands in the Cherokee Nation's domain east of the Mississippi River. Even though this treaty was negotiated by a non-elected group of Cherokees, the officials of Georgia, and President Andrew Jackson, John Ross, the duly elected leader of the Cherokees was forced to accept the removal treaty as a reality on May 23, 1836, when the United States Senate ratified the New Echota Treaty by one vote.

This act by the removal treaty committee meant sure death for the principals who signed the treaty according to Cherokee doctrine which made non-sanctioned land cessions punishable by death. The inevitable happened and John Ross' party was held responsible. John Ridge, Major Ridge, and Elias Boudinot were assassinated on June 22, 1839. Their deaths made for increased tension among the Cherokees but the event did not prevent the Cherokees, now in Indian Territory, from forming and signing a new constitution on September 6, 1839.

John Ross' bid for power among the Cherokees was never completely resolved among the Cherokees in Indian Territory, until a complete government investigation headed by Colonel Roger Jones. The treaty of August 6, 1846, finally united the Cherokees, at least on paper.

The Cherokee nation prospered until the Civil War. When this conflict broke out, Ross tried for the position of neutrality, but it was a difficult position for a man who was himself a slave owner. For whatever reasons, Ross eventually endorsed the Confederacy position. There was again confusion in the Cherokee Nation since one faction believed in the Union and joined the Union side. There was civil war in the Cherokee Nation as well as in the United States. This was probably the final straw that broke the Cherokee Nation as a nation. It was never to be the same.

John Ross never saw the disorder of the reconstruction period. He died on August 1, 1866, after having been with the Cherokees as principal chief for 38 years.

ROUNDHEAD (Wyandot; fl. 19th century), like Tecumseh and several other chiefs, fought on the side of the British against the United States during the War of 1812. A handsome and well-known Wyandot chief, Roundhead met his death during the opening year of the war, after urging British military commanders to fight the Americans more aggressively.

RUNNING ANTELOPE (Dakota) had his portrait on the 1899 issue of the $5 silver certificate.

RUSHING BEAR (Arikara) was also known as *Son of Star*.

□ □ □

Rain-in-the-Face

Rantchewaime

Red Cloud

Red Fish

Red Jacket

Red Tomahawk

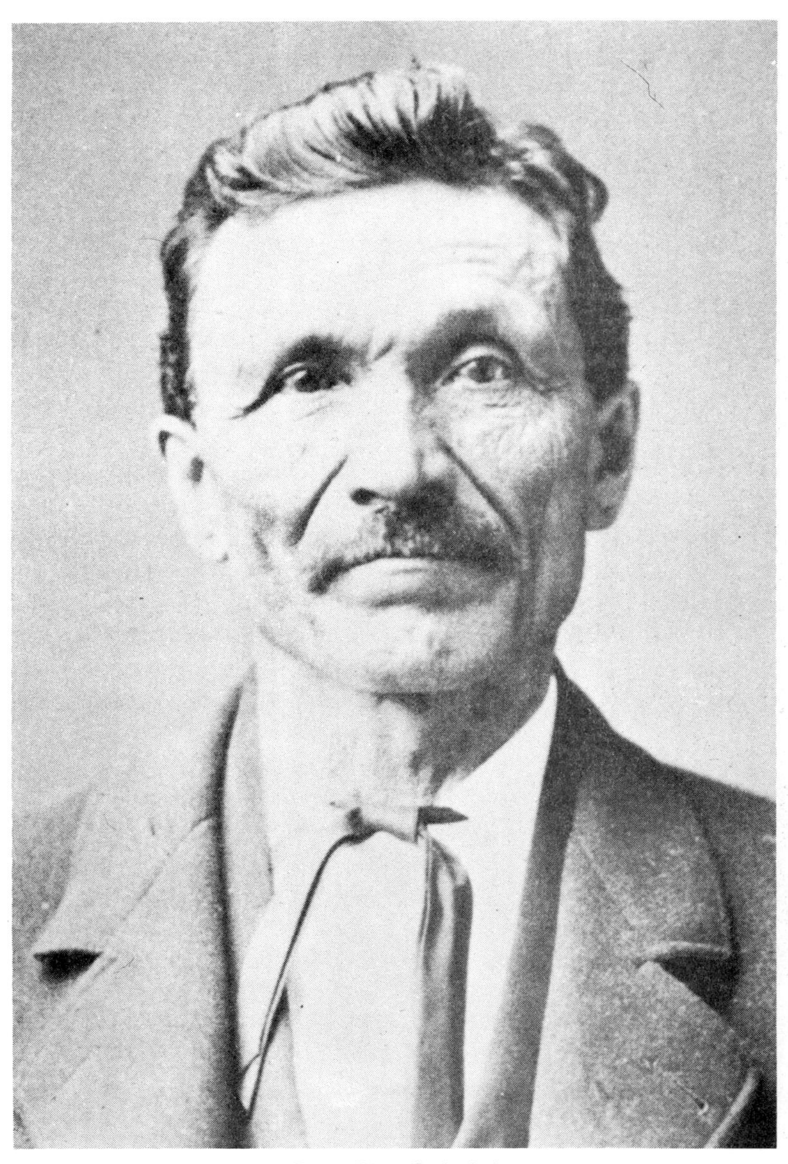

Renville, Gabriel

Revenger

Reynolds, Allie

Riddle, Toby

Ridge, John Rollin

Ridge, Major

Running Antelope

Rushing Bear

S

SABEATA (Jumano; fl. 17th century), informed Spanish officials of "the great kingdom of the Texas" and later accompanied the expedition under Domingo de Mendoza to the interior of Texas in 1683– 84. Leader of a tribe living at the mouth of the Rio Conchos in Chihuahua, Sabeata went to Paso del Norte, Texas in October 1683 to ask the Spanish governor there to provide missions for the Jumano and to protect his people from the Apache. During the Mendoza expedition, however, he had a falling out with the Spaniards and departed. Years later he was encountered while on a buffalo hunt, still carrying his Spanish commission and still requesting additional missions for his people.

SACAJAWEA (Shoshoni; *c.* 1787—April 9, 1884), was a Shoshoni Indian who became well-known to whites as a guide and interpreter for the explorers William Clark and Meriwether Lewis. She accompanied their expedition from present-day North Dakota to the Pacific Ocean and back, caring for her infant son born about two months before the expedition left her village. Controversy surrounds her later years. She may have died when about 25 years old, or may have lived to become a respected counselor before her death at nearly 100.

Sacajawea was born about 1787, probably in western Montana or eastern Idaho where her tribe, the Shoshoni, roamed. She did not become known to white people until 1804, when she was living in a Mandan village on the Missouri River near present-day Bismarck, North Dakota. As later became known, when she was about 14, she and another girl had been captured by the Hidatsa Indians (a tribe closely related to the Mandan), and taken far east of their tribe's homeland. The other girl later escaped, but Sacajawea was left with the Hidatsa. Sometime after her capture, she was bought by a French-Canadian fur trader, Toussaint

Charbonneau who lived with the Indians. Charbonneau made her one of his wives.

Sacajawea became known to white people through contact with the Lewis and Clark Expedition, sent by Pres. Thomas Jefferson to explore the newly purchased Louisiana Territory and make contact with the Native Americans there. Since that time, there has been some controversy over the spelling of her name and its English translation. Sacajawea is a commonly accepted spelling and *Bird Woman* a commonly accepted meaning, although Meriwether Lewis and William Clark spelled her name several ways, and Sacajawea has also been translated *Boat Woman*. One explanation is that the key element in her name is associated with motion and doesn't necessarily have anything to do with either birds or boats.

Lewis and Clark arrived at the village where Sacajawea lived in the summer of 1804 and wintered there. When they left the next year, it was with Charbonneau and Sacajawea. Some historians believe that, although the explorers let Charbonneau believe his skills were required by the expedition, they were really interested in taking Sacajawea with them as interpreter when they passed westwards through the lands of her people, and as living proof to the Indians they would meet that their intentions were peaceful. Another viewpoint is that Charbonneau, as a mountain man experienced with Indians, was also desired by the expedition. There is some dispute as to Sacajawea's legendary acclaim as guide; it is possible that since she was under 14 when she left the Rocky Mountain homeland of her tribe, she may not have remembered enough to guide the explorers, but she proved indispensable to the expedition in other ways, and the journals of Lewis and Clark provide a running record of the admiration and affection which they felt for her.

On February 11, 1805, Lewis wrote in his journal: "About five o'clock this evening one of the wives of

Charbonon was delivered of a fine boy, it is worthy of remark that this was the first child this woman had boarn, and as common in such cases her labour was tedious and the pain violent." (Wissler, *Indians of the United States*, p. 233) Sacajawea took her young son Baptiste with her, strapped to her back, when the expedition started up the Missouri River on April 7, 1805. She soon proved her usefulness as a food provider, as the following quote from Lewis' journal on April 9 shows. He says that when the expedition stopped for dinner, Sacajawea "busied herself in search for the wild artichokes which the mice (gophers?) collect and deposit in large hordes. This operation she performed by penetrating the earth with a sharp stick about some collection of driftwood. Her labors soon proved successful and she procured a good quantity of these roots." (Hebard, *Sacajawea,* p. 52.) Later, she was to find them edible fennel and a plant whose root "resembled a carrot in form and size and something of its colour, but a paler yellow than that of our carrot." (Hebard, *Sacajawea*, p. 79.)

On May 14, Sacajawea proved she could do more than find food and interpret. Clark describes the incident, which occurred near the Yellowstone River, in the following way: "We proceeded on very well until about six o'clock. A squall of wind struck our sail broadside and turned the perogue nearly over, and in this situation the perogue remained until the sail was cut down, in which time she nearly filled with water. The articles which floated out were nearly all caught by the squaw who was in the rear. This accident had like to have cost us dearly; for in this perogue were embarked our papers, instruments, books, medicine, a great proportion of our merchandise, and, in short, almost every article indispensibly necessary to further the views and insure the success of the enterprise in which we are now launched to the distance of 2,200 miles." (Hebard, *Sacajawea*, p. 52-3.) In his own journal, Lewis adds, "The Indian woman, to whom I ascribe equal fortitude and resolution with any person on board at the time of the accident, caught and preserved most of the light articles which were washed overboard." (Hebard, *Sacajawea*, p. 53.) On May 20, the explorers gave a river Sacajawea's name.

On June 10, Sacajawea became ill. Two days later, Clark "moved her into the back part of our covered part of the perogue, which is cool, her own situation being a very hot one in the bottom of the perogue exposed to the sun." (Hebard, *Sacajawea*, p. 55.) She was bled several times by Clark, and was completely recovered by June 24, but only after having suffered a relapse on June 18, caused, Lewis was sure, by her intemperate feasting on raw white apples and dried fish. On June 29, a flash flood almost drowned Sacajawea, her baby, Clark, his black servant York, and Charbonneau, but Clark's quick action reduced the loss to a gun and other small equipment. Towards the end of July, the expedition entered country Sacajawea recognized as her homeland. On August 8, as Lewis wrote, "The Indian woman recognized the point of high plain to our right, which she informed us was not very distant from the summer retreat of her nation on a river beyond the mountains which runs to the west. This hill she says her nation calls the beaver's head from a conceived resemblance of its figure to the head of that animal. She assures us that we shall either find her people on this river or on the river immediately west of it's source." (Hebard, *Sacajawea*, p. 61.) Shortly afterwards, there was an unpleasant incident in which Charbonneau was discovered mistreating Sacajawea, but Clark reprimanded him, and apparently did not see him again strike his wife.

In the middle of August, the expedition met up with Sacajawea's tribe. Chief of the tribe was a man named Cameahwait. In one of the expedition's journals the following meeting is described: "After this, the conference was to be opened, and glad of an opportunity of being able to converse more intelligibly, Sacajawea was sent for; she came into the tent, sat down, and was beginning to interpret, when in the person of Cameahwait she recognized her brother; she instantly jumped up and ran and embraced him, throwing over him her blanket and weeping profusely; the chief himself was moved, though not in the same degree. After some conversation between them she resumed her seat, and attempted to interpret for us, but her new situation seemed to overpower her, and she was frequently interrupted by her tears. After the council was finished the unfortunate woman learned that all her family were dead except two brothers, one of whom was absent, and a son of her eldest sister, a small boy, who was immediately adopted by her." (Hebard, *Sacajawea*, p. 67). While in the land of the Shoshoni, Sacajawea was instrumental in assuring the expedition got enough horses to cross the Rocky Mountains that fall. Without her timely help, Lewis and Clark must either have lost half a year camping east of the Rockies, or continued underprovided. It was not in the plans of Lewis and Clark to take Sacajawea the final few miles to the Pacific Ocean, but Sacajawea heard that a whale had been found on the beach, and as Lewis wrote on January 6, 1806: "The Indian woman was very importunate to be permitted to go, and was therefore indulged; she observed that she had traveled along way with us to see the great waters, and that now that monstrous fish was also to be seen, she thought it very hard she could not be permitted to see either (she had never yet been to the Ocean). (Wissler, *Indians of the United States*, p. 234.) Returning that spring back across the Rockies, Sacajawea provided great help as an interpreter and a guide. Clark wrote on July 13, "The Indian woman, has been of great service to me as a pilot through this country, recommends a gap in the mountains more south which I shall cross." (Herbard, *Sacajawea*, p. 79.)

When the expedition returned to the Mandan villages, Sacajawea remained there with her baby and her husband, but Clark had so fallen in love with the little boy, when he called "my little dancing boy" and nicknamed *Pomp*, that he offered to raise and educate him in the United States. Sacajawea and her husband did not accept his offer immediately, but there are indications that in 1811 they may have journeyed to St. Louis to give Baptiste over into the care of Clark.

Here is where controversy over the course of Sacajawea's life sets in. Some historians maintain that she died in 1812. Chief evidence for this belief is an entry dated December 20, 1812, in the journal of a fur trader named John C. Luttig, who in 1813 was appointed temporary guardian of two of Sacajawea's children. The entry states: "Clear and moderate. . . . This evening the Wife of Charbonneau, a Snake Squaw died of a putrid fever she was a good and the best Women in the fort, aged about 25 years she left a fine infant girl." (Wessler, *Indians of the United States*, p. 236.) Other historians, chief among them Grace Raymond Hebard (*Sacajawea. . .*, 1932), maintain that Luttig's entry referred to another Shoshoni wife of Charbonneau, and that Sacajawea had actually remained in St. Louis to help Clark care for her six year old son Baptiste. It is said that Baptiste was educated in St. Louis by Clark and that he later became an interpreter and mountain man, then traveled widely in Europe as a favorite of Prince Paul of Wurttemburg, finally returning and dying in the American West, apparently among the Shoshoni. Hebard attributes the fact that he was never adopted by Clark, although court records show that Clark did adopt Toussaint and Lizette, the young son and daughter of Charbonneau, to the fact that Sacajawea must have been living in St. Louis at the time and was responsible for her son.

Based on some documents, the work of other researchers, and many interviews, Hebard constructed the following outline of Sacajawea's life after 1812. Sometime before 1820, Charbonneau collected his wife in St. Louis and took her to what is now western Oklahoma and Kansas. There friction developed between Sacajawea and a young Ute woman Charbonneau had recnetly wed. Charbonneau beat Sacajawea, whereupon she left him to live among the Comanche Indians. There she married Jerk Meat and bore five children, two of whom lived. When Jerk Meat was killed in a battle, Sacajawea disappeared from the Comanche and returned north to her Shoshoni people, talking with her Yaga-wosier, or Crying Basket, her young daughter. In reference to her unexplained disappearance, her name in Comanche tradition became *Wedze-wipe* or *Lost woman.*

According to Hebard, Sacajawea made it back to her Shoshoni tribe in about 1850, where she was well taken care of by her adopted son Bazil, or Shoo-gan, who had become a respected sub-chief of the tribe. Hebard believes that Sacajawea played an important behind-the-scenes role in tribal decisions, counseling strongly for peace with the whites. At this time she acquired a new name, Porivo or chief. She also may have served as interpreter between Indian agents to have encouraged the Shoshoni to adopt the farming methods urged by the federal government. In 1871, she moved to the newly created Wind River Reservation in west-central Wyoming. There she died on April 9, 1884.

SACKETT, JOHN (Athabascan; June 3, 1944–), became the youngest representative ever elected to the Alaska Legislature. Educated at Ohio University and the University of Alaska, Sackett also served as treasurer of the Alaska Federation of Natives, vice-president of the Fairbanks Native Association, and as president of the Tanana Chiefs.

SADEKANATIE (Onondaga; fl. late 17th and early 18th centuries), a principal chief of the Onondaga, spoke at various tribal councils and represented his people to government officials at Albany. He first spoke on behalf of his tribe at a council meeting on January 29, 1690 at Onondaga, New York. Sadekanatie went to Albany in 1693 and 1700, the latter time despite his fears of being poisoned. The Onondaga chief died in 1701.

SADEKANATIE (Onondaga; fl. 18th century), succeeded the first Onondaga chief of that name. He assumed leadership of the tribe in 1701 and signed land deeds that year and in 1726. Although he never attained the prominence of his predecessor in tribal councils, the second Sadekanatie did make two extended speeches at Albany in August 1710.

SAGAUNASH (Potawatomi; *c.* 1780—September 28, 1741), known to the British as Billy Caldwell, was a Potawatomi sub-chief born 1780 in Canada, who supported Tecumseh during the War of 1812 but later served the U.S. His father, William Caldwell, was an Irish soldier in the British army, and his mother was Potawatomi. Educated in Roman Catholic schools in Detroit, he could read and write French and English, and understood several Indian dialects. Sagaunash urged his people to learn from the white way of life, and he maintained a belief in the necessity to educate Indian youth.

A strong supporter of Tecumseh, Sagaunash opposed the U.S. and the encroachments of white settlers, but also fought unnecessary cruelties toward whites. Arriving at Fort Dearborn a day after the August 15, 1812 massacre, he may have helped prevent further slaughter. He served as Tecumseh's interpreter and secretary, and was with him at the Battle of the Thames (October, 1813). Remaining in Canada after the war, Sagaunash was given the title of *captain of the Indian Department* by the British.

In 1820, Sagaunash moved to the Chicago area, and swore his allegiance to the U.S. His loyalty to the government was always above suspicion, and in

1826 he was given the office of justice of the peace. During the Winnebago outbreak of 1827, Sagaunash assisted the U.S. and aided in the subsequent treaty settlements. The following year, at the mouth of the Chicago River, the government built him a house which may have been the first frame structure in the area.

Dissuading the younger members of his tribe from joining Black Hawk's warriors in 1832, Sagaunash participated in the resulting treaties, and in 1833, with the rest of the Potawatomi nation, ceded all lands east of the Mississippi to the U.S. In 1836 he removed to western Iowa where he died at Council Bluffs, September 28, 1841.

SAGHWAREESA (Tuscarora; fl. 18th century), was an influential chief of the Tuscarora during the middle of the 18th century. Already prominent by 1750, Saghwareesa met with Sir William Johnson (Minister for North American Indian Affairs) at Oneida Lake in 1761. In 1768, the chief signed the Fort Stanwix treaty on behalf of the Tuscarora.

SAGONAQUADE (Onondaga and Tuscarora; 1846– ?), also Albert Cusick lost his opportunity to become a chief because he was a Christian, but devoted his life to performing good works for the Tuscarora. Sagonaquade was a descendent of a Tuscarora chief, but his mother was an Onondaga. Ordained a deacon in 1891, he devoted himself to religious works on the reservation. Sagonaquade also assisted in various studies of Indian language and folklore.

SAINTE-MARIE, BUFFY (Cree, February 20 1941 or 1942 –), popular Cree folksinger and recording artist, was born on the Piapot Reserve in Craven, Saskatchewan, Canada, on February 20, in 1941 or 1942. She was orphaned as an infant and adopted by a part-Micmac Indian couple, Albert and Winifred Sainte-Marie. Buffy grew up in Wakefield, Massachusetts, as a United States citizen. As a small child she learned to play the piano and at an early age wrote poems that she set to her own music. At age 17 she learned to play the guitar.

Buffy enrolled at the University of Massachusetts to study veterinary science but switched to education and philosophy. She also took courses at Smith, Mt. Holyoke, and Amherst colleges. Before graduating from the University of Massachusetts in 1963 she had become popular as a campus and coffee-house folk-singer. She moved to New York and began performing at clubs in Greenwich Village. An immediate hit, she decided to turn professional.

By 1965 Buffy Sainte-Marie was performing at Carnegie Hall in New York, the Newport Folk Festival in Rhode Island, and Royal Albert Hall in London. Soon the widely acclaimed artist was appearing in cities all over the United States and the world. In 1964 she turned out *It's My Way*, the first of many record albums. Many of Buffy's songs are her own. They have included city blues like *Broke-down Girl*, love songs like *Until It's Time for You to Go*, country tunes like *Cripple Creek*, the personal drug-withdrawal experience told in *Cod'ine*, anti-war songs like *The Universal Soldier*, and Indian protest songs like *My Country 'Tis of Thy People You're Dying* and *Now That the Buffalo's Gone*. She usually accompanies herself on a guitar and sometimes she uses a Creek Indian mouth bow.

Buffy had had no voice training until after the start of her career. She sings in a low and husky, hauntingly intense style. In addition to her singing career, Buffy has written poetry, lectured and written on Indian history and culture, and acted on TV. In 1966 she was named to the advisory council for the Upward Bound program of the Office of Economic Opportunity. In 1969 she performed for the Poor People's Campaign in Washington, D.C. Buffy married Dewain Kamaikalani Bugbee, a man of mixed American Indian, Hawaiian, and European ancestry, in 1967.

SAKAWESTON (?; fl. 17th century) was kidnapped in 1611 from an island off the New England coast. He spent many years living in England, where he had been taken by his captor—a Captain Harlow. Then, according to an account by Captain John Smith, Sakaweston went to Bohemia as a soldier to fight in the seventeenth century European wars.

SAMOSET (Pemaquid; *c.* 1600–1653), had learned some English expressions from coastal traders, enabling him to startle the newly landed Pilgrims in March 1620 when he walked into their camp and said, "Welcome Englishmen, Welcome Englishmen." When the Pilgrims first saw Samoset, the Pemaquid was in a state of destitution. Undoubtedly weakened by the plague that had decimated the coastal tribes from 1615 to 1617, Samoset had been in the Cape Cod area for about eight months prior to the Mayflower's arrival. The Pilgrims gave the haggard native a coat and some food, thereby initiating an era of friendly and profitable Indian relationships for the European immigrants.

Samoset soon left the Plymouth colony, only to return a short time later leading a band of Wampanoag warriors, including their chief Massasoit. Another English-speaking native, named Squanto, was in the group, and Squanto stayed with the Pilgrims to teach them how to survive in the wilderness. Perhaps more important in terms of the future, Massasoit agreed to an alliance with the white settlers that would result in huge tracts of territory going over to the English. Samoset himself sold a great deal of land; in fact, it was Samoset who executed the first deed made between the Indians and the English. In July 1625, Samoset sold 12,000 acres of Pemaquid territory to John Brown of New Harbor.

There is no historical record of Samoset's activities from the 1625 deed to another land transaction in 1653. In that year, the Pemaquid sagamore signed over 1000 acres to William Parnell, Thomas Way, and William England. Samoset died soon afterwards, and he was buried in the town of Bristol, the land once occupied solely by his ancestors. He is, of course, remembered (like Squanto) as the friendly native who saved the colonists in their time of greatest need. Samoset failed to comprehend, however, that his generosity in terms of land cessions to the whites would doom his people's continued existence on their tribal territory.

SANTANTAS (Kiowa) was the son of Satanta.

SASSABA (Chippewa; fl. 18th century), also known as The Count and as Myeengun, was a minor Chippewa chief of the Crane branch. He and his brother fought under Tecumseh at the Battle of the Thames, Canada, Aug. 5, 1813. His brother's death in this battle developed in Sassaba an intense hatred toward the Americans that was never mollified. In 1820 Gen. Lewis Cass travelled to Sault Ste. Marie for negotiations with the Chippewa chiefs to purchase a small tract of land for the erection of a garrison. In a council of chiefs attended by Sassaba, Cass informed him that the garrison would be built with or without Chippewa permission. Sassaba angrily replied that the land would never be sold, refused the peace pipe, rejected the gifts presented by Cass, threw down the war lance, and rushed to his tent where he hoisted the British flag. Cass responded by calmly ripping the flag down. Because two of the chiefs were convinced by the daughter of another that Cass would not hesitate to use arms in Chippewa territory, the conference was resumed. Sassaba left the conference. Within two hours a treaty was signed.

SASSACUS (Pequot; 1560– 1637), perhaps the same as Massachusetts *Sassakusu*,'he is wild', was the noted and last important chief of the Pequot tribe. He was the son and successor of Wopigwooit, the first chief of the tribe whom the whites had come in contact, was killed by the Dutch, about 1632, at or near the site of Hartford, Conn., then the principal Pequot settlement. Soon after becoming chief in Oct. 1634 Sassacus sent an emissary to the governor of the Massachusetts Bay colony to ask for a treaty of friendship, offering as an inducement to surrender all the rights of the Pequot to the lands they had conquered, provided the colonists settle a plantation among his people. It was an offer which he must have known he could not carry out, and perhaps had no intention of trying to fulfill, as he nourished bitter enmity toward the whites. This proposal had the effect of turning Uncus, the Mohegan chief, against him. The domain of the Pequot during Sassacus's leadership extended from Narragansett Bay to Hudson and included the larger part of Long Island, and it is said that at the height of his prosperity no fewer than 26 sachems were subordinate to him. Because of his depredations especially on the neighboring tribes, the colonists decided in 1636 to make war on the Pequot. The name of Sassacus had inspired such terror among the surrounding tribes that the Indian allies of the whites could not believe the latter would dare to make a direct attack on the stronghold of this wily chief. The war was soon ended, and Sassacus, having suffered defeat and the loss of a large portion of his people, fled with 20 or 30 of his warriors to the Mohawk country. Even here he found no safety, for before the close of 1637 his scalp and those of his brother and five other Pequot chiefs were sent to the governor of Massachusetts by the Mohawk. As Sassacus had carried with him in his flight a large quantity of wampum, a desire on the part of the Mohawk to possess this treasure may have led to his death and that his followers.

SATANTA (Kiowa; *c.* 1820– October 11, 1878), Indian name Set-tain-te, ("White Bear") was a Kiowa chief revered to this day by his people as one of their greatest men. For his eloquence in council he was acclaimed "Orator of the Plains." His ability to combine directness of purpose with grace and wit won the admiration of army officers, even though he was known to be hostile to white laws and white civilization. He was a merciless killer because he knew there was no other way to retain Kiowa lands.

Satanta was one of nine signers of the Medicine Lodge Creek Treaty, Barber County, Kansas, October 21, 1867, by which the Kiowas agreed to live on a reservation. In reality, he had no intention of signing away his freedom, but the military might of the United States proved too much for the Indians. Winter was upon them; they were cold and hungry.

Under a white flag of truce, Satanta and Lone Wolf came to General Philip Sheridan's camp to tell him of their decision to move their people to the Fort Cobb agency in Oklahoma. General George A. Custer, who went out to meet the pair, was so hostile that all the Kiowas hovering in the background ran away. Custer took the chiefs as hostages until the runaways returned. They did, but the Kiowas, especially the young braves, found reservation life unbearable. Even Satanta participated in a raid into Texas in May 1871, during which the warriors attacked a wagon train and killed seven teamsters.

Back on the reservation, Satanta and three other chiefs were called before General William T. Sherman, who put them under arrest and told them that they would be returned to Texas to stand trial for murder. Lone Wolf escaped then; Setangya (Sitting Bear) was killed on the way to Texas, so that only Satanta and Big Tree were tried and sentenced to death by hanging. Indian agents arranged to have the sentence changed to life imprisonment. Satanta's friends brought about his release, but immediately he participated in new raids. Recaptured, he was sent to prison at Huntsville. Two years later he jumped from a second-floor window to his death.

SAUL, C. TERRY (Choctaw-Chickasaw; April 2, 1921–   ), as both a commercial illustrator and an independent artist, has created works that appear in museums and private collections around the world. After receiving his Bachelor of Fine Arts (1948) and Master of Fine Arts (1949) degrees from the University of Oklahoma, Saul opened his own studio — the Village Arts Studio — in New York City. Later, he worked as a technical illustrator and staff artist for Curtis-Wright in Garfield, New Jersey and as a comercial artist for Phillips Petroleum Company back in his native Oklahoma.

Saul's paintings have won him recognition and acclaim throughout the country. He has been commissioned to do many paintings and murals, and his one-man and group shows have earned him numerous awards — including the Special Indian Artists award. His reputation has spread beyond the boundaries of the United States, and Saul's paintings can presently be seen in Austria, Germany, Denmark, and The Netherlands.

SAVILLA, AGNESS (Mohave; *c.* 1910–   ), became the first woman elected to the Colorado River Tribal Council. After attending the Haskell Institute, Agness Savilla taught school on the Navaho reservation for many years. Then, in 1943, she was elected to the Tribal Council, where she served until 1968. Following her retirement from politics, Savilla continued to serve as Chairman of the Council's Health, Education and Welfare Committee. In addition, she held the post of regional vice-president of the National Congress of American Indians and acted as U.S. delegate to the 1964 Inter-American Congress on Indians at Quito, Ecuador.

SAYENQUERAGHTA (Seneca; fl. 18th century), although not an elected or hereditary chief, signed several treaties on behalf of the Seneca during the latter half of the 18th century. Sayenqueraghta was a chief because the British government declared him so and the Seneca accepted him as such. He signed the Eston treaty in 1758; the treaty of Johnson Hall (New York) on April 3, 1764; and he participated in tribal councils as well as in those of the Six Nations until 1775. He died sometime before 1788.

SCARFACED CHARLEY (Modoc; 1839–1888), was the brilliant military leader of the Modoc forces in their 1872-73 war against removal to the Klamath Reservation. Said by historians to have possessed the best military and engineering capabilities on both sides during the war, he nevertheless consistently attempted to persuade his fellow tribesmen to avoid bloodshed. He was known by Modoc and American alike both for his battlefield genius and compassion and mercy he displayed toward a helpless foe.

Scarfaced Charley was born in Northeastern California. As a young man he worked occasionally for a white rancher named Fairchild, and there he learned to speak English. In 1861 he participated in a raid on a wagon train which was passing illegally through Modoc territory near Lost River, and by 1870 he had become virtually the first lieutenant of Kintpuash, a band sub-chief. His nickname derived from a long, deep scar on his face, the result of a wagon accident he had as a boy.

Like most other Modocs, Scarfaced Charley found conditions on the Klamath Reservation, to which the tribe had been removed, unbearable, and so joined Kintpuash when he returned to Lost River. When hostilities erupted and the Modocs retreated to the Lava Flats to make a stand, Scarfaced Charley stopped on route to warn several white ranchers to go home so that they would be out of danger.

In battle, however, he was a force to be reckoned with. Historian Richard Dillon states that his ambush and decimation of an American force led by Captain Evan Thomas "was perhaps the most perfect entrapment of troops in Indian war history. He utterly smashed a force three times the size of his own and within three miles of the field head-quarters of the army." After this victory had been won, however, he restrained his forces and permitted any surviving troopers to depart in safety. "All you fellows that ain't dead had better go home," he said. "We don't want to kill you all in one day!"

Scarfaced Charley did not actively participate in the assassination of General Canby and his party. Rather, he extended his protection to the translators, Frank and Toby Riddle, thus providing for their survival.

Scarfaced Charley surrendered only after the combined might of the American forces and the treachery of Modocs like Hooker Jim crushed the Modoc resistance. He was, though officially pardoned, exiled with other Modoc warriors and their families to the Quapaw Agency in Indian Territory. After a brief tour with A.B. Meacham's travelling show on the Modoc War, he returned there and for a short time served as "chief" of the group. In 1888 he died of tuberculosis, never having been permitted to return to his native land.

SCAROUADY (Oneida; fl. 18th century), also Half King, chief of the Oneida Indians in western Pennsylvania, allied himself and his tribe firmly with the English colonists during the British-French imperial conflicts of the 1750's. Scarouady hated the French, and to escape their influence he moved from Logstown to Aughwick, Pennsylvania in 1754. There he assumed command over the western Pennsylvania Oneida, succeeding Half-King Scruniyatha.

A great orator — frequently the leading speaker at intertribal conferences — Scarouady summoned all his considerable talent in May 1754 to urge the Indians of Fort Cumberland to accompany the British expedition under General Braddock on its ill-fated march against the alliance of French and Indians along the western frontier. By 1756, however, the Oneida chief was making speeches advocating peace; one such speech occured on July 1, 1756 before Sir William Johnson — British representative to the North American tribes — at a conference of the Six Nations.

SCHEIRBECK, HELEN M. (Lumbee; August 21, 1935–   ), in serving as director of HEW's Education for American Indians Office, has worked closely with many tribes and native organizations in an effort to improve educational and economic opportunities for Indian young people. After receiving her B.A. degree from Berea College, Helen M. Scheirbeck seved as director of the Center for Action on Poverty at the University of Wisconsin, consultant to the Office of Economic Opportunity, and associate director of the Office of Community Development in the Bureau of Indian Affairs. As a member of the staff of the U.S. Senate's Sub-Committee on Constitutional Rights, she was largely responsible for hearings on Indian rights being held throughout the country; one consequence of these hearings was the passage of the Indian Bill of Rights as a section of the Civil Rights Act of 1968.

SCHONCHIN (Modoc; *c.* 1811– *c.* 1870s), known also as Sconchin or Old Schonchin, was the last full-tribal chief of the Modocs. Though a bitter and consistent enemy of white incursion into Modoc territory in his youth, he honored a peace treaty which he signed in 1864 and did not participate in the Modoc War of 1872-73. Throughout the latter part of his life he acted as major spokesman for the inhabitants of the Modoc sub-agency at Yainax on the Klamath Reservation in Oregon.

Schonchin was born about 1811 near the upper bend of the Link River in Oregon. Little is known of his early life, though he is said to have gained tribal chieftainship in 1845 more through his ability as a warrior and orator than through his family lineage.

In 1854 illness kept him from attending the Modoc peace delegation which was massacred by the Siskiyou County Rangers under Ben Wright, but the lesson of white treachery did not escape him.

By 1860, with many of the tribe's leaders and young men slain, Schonchin led his people in suing for peace. He bitterly characterized the whites for their apparent inability to distinguish the by-then peaceful Modoc from the more bellicose Snake and Pit River, and concluded in frustration, "I think if we kill all white men, no more come. We kill and kill but, all time, more come and more come like grass in spring. I throw down my gun. I say 'I will fight no more.' My heart is sick. I am old man."

In 1864 Schonchin, representing 339 Modoc, agreed by treaty to remove the tribe to a portion of the newly created Klamath Reservation well to the north of Modoc territory. There the tribe experienced a variety of deprivations. The Klamath's outnumbered Schonchin's people two to one and treated them with contempt. Food supplies promised by treaty failed to arrive and hunger and malnutrition were prevalent.

Some Modocs, principally those in the band led by Kintpuash, felt that the American government in failing to keep its part of the bargain had nullified the treaty. After a year they left Klamath and returned to their former homes along the Lost River, though Sconchin and the majority of the tribe remained in Oregon. Four years later a reconciliation was attempted by A.M. Meacham, Superintendant for Indian Affairs in Oregon. The dissident band returned but relations with the Klamath did not improve and Modoc complaints were ignored by the local Indian Agent who, in 1870, cut off all food supplies to the tribe.

This time the entire Modoc Nation left the reservation, causing the Indian Bureau to develop at last a realistic solution to the problem. A separate Modoc agency was established on the reservation at Yainax, some 35 miles distant from the previously assigned Modoc territory. Schonchin and the majority of the tribe were willing to try again and returned to the reservation. Kintpuash and his followers refused to come back, a decision which paved the way for the armed hostilities which followed some two years later.

During the Modoc War, Schonchin and most of the Yainax band remained neutral. The old chief, who continued in his office until the late 1870s, exerted his leadership in preventing a spread of the fighting, but was less successful in negotiating a return of Kintpuash's band.

SCHONCHIN JOHN (Modoc; 1839–1874), was the younger brother of Schonchin, last full tribal chief of the Modocs, and himself a sub-chief or *sajint* of a small band. Together with Kintpuash and Scarfaced Charlie, he led the resistance in the Modoc War of 1872-73. A cynical and eloquant spokesman, he urged and participated in the assasination of General Canby and his Commission in 1873. Captured toward the end of the hostilities, he was tried, convicted and executed at Fort Klamath in1874.

Born near the upper bend of the Link River in Oregon, Schonchin John did not assume a leadership role in the tribe until 1872. He accompanied Kintpuash when the Chief left the Klamath Reservation for the former Modoc territory near Lost River, and was consistently an advocate for armed resistance against American efforts to remove the Modocs back to Klamath.

At one tribal council he declared that peace with the whites was impossible and stated, "I have been trapped and fooled by the white people many times. I do not intend to be fooled again. You will see the aim of the Peace Commission. They are just leading us Mucklucks on, to make time to get more soldiers here. When they think there are enough men here, they will jump on us and kill the last soul of us. . . ."

He strongly argued in favor of the assasination of the Commission led by General Canby, and himself shot the Superintendant of Indian Affairs for Oregon, A.B. Meacham, though the latter survived. He was one of the last of the Modocs to surrender, and was promptly charged and tried for murder. As with the five other defendants, he was given no legal counsel, and his conviction was never in doubt.

Schonchin John was pronounced guilty and sentenced to hang along with Kintpuash, Boston Charlie and Black Jim. After the execution, his corpse was decapitated, scalped and defleshed, and his skull sent to the archives of the Smithsonian Institute in Washington, D.C. Listed as inventory item #1019, it reposes there to this day.

SEATTLE (Squamish; 1790– 1866), Squamish Indian chief, lives on not only in Washington's largest city, but in its State history, which records him as "the greatest Indian friend white settlers ever had."

Seattle, son of Chief Schweabe, witnessed as a boy the (1792) arrival in Puget Sound of the British explorer Vancouver and his men, in their "immense white-winged bird ship," the *Discovery*. The new riches, and the first white men he had ever seen, profoundly impressed Seattle, who became convinced as he grew up that peace, not war, was the right path for men to follow.

It was a revolutionary belief. Battle and pillaging were a long-established way of life among Pacific Coast Indians, and as a young man, Seattle planned and led an alliance of six tribes against "horse tribes" to the northeast. Although his success in the undertaking won the young chief the high position of "Chief of the Allied Tribes" (the Dwamish Confederacy), it was his last feat as a warrior. Seattle devoted the rest of his life to promoting peace.

When Catholic missionaries entered the Northwest in the 1830's, Seattle became a convert to Christianity and took the baptismal name "Noah," after his favorite Bilical character. He inaugurated regular morning and evening prayers among his people, a practice they continued after his death.

Seattle had ample opportunity to demonstrate his belief in brotherhood. White settlers who founded a small community on Puget Sound in 1851 received unlimited friendship and help from him, and shared his people's fish, seafood, and venison. In 1852, the little settlement which had first been hopefully called "New York," and later "Alki Point," was renamed, for all time, "Seattle."

But as more white immigrants came to the Northwest, relations with the Indians became strained and stormy. During the winter of 1854-55, several northwest tribes organized in the hope of driving whites out of the country. In January 1855, Washington Territory's first Governor and Superintendent of Indian Affairs, Isaac I. Stevens, called Seattle's bands together, and told them of plans for a treaty which would place them on reservations.

Seattle, over 6 feet tall, broad-shouldered, deep-chested, an impressive and powerful orator, replied to the Governor in a resounding voice which all his people assembled along the beach could hear. According to a white spectator's translation, the dignified old leader's words, although marked by sadness and resignation, were poetic. They are said to have gone, in part:

"Whatever I say, the Great Chief at Washington can rely on," Seattle said. "His people are many, like grass that covers vast prairies. Our people once covered the land as waves of a wind-ruffled sea cover its shell-paved floor, but now my people are few.

"Our great and good Father sends us word that if we do as he desires he will buy our lands . . . allow us to live comfortably . . . protect us with his brave warriors; his wonderful ships of war will fill our harbors. Then our ancient northern enemies will cease to frighten our women, children and old men.

"But day and night can not dwell together. The red man has ever fled the approach of the white man as morning mist flees the rising sun. It matters little where we pass the remnant of our days. They will not be many. The Indian's night promises to be dark . . . a few more moons . . . a few more winters."

Seattle was the first signer of the Port Elliott Treaty of 1855 which placed Washington tribes on reservations.

But in the wake of the new treaties, several Indian groups, placed on reservation lands which did not include hunting or fishing areas, opened attack on white settlers. "Horse" tribes of eastern Washington combined to lead a war in which they tried to enlist "canoe" Indians. Some coastal tribes did join the alliance, but Seattle's followers remained generally loyal to whites and were evacuated in sloops and canoes to Port Madison Reservation. Throughout this and other Indian wars of the period, Seattle faithfully supported the white cause, at the same time continuing to be a true and powerful leader of his own people.

In line with the tribal belief that mention of a dead man's name disturbs his spirit, Seattle levied a small tribute in advance upon the citizens of the new town named after him. At about 76, he died on Port Madison Reservation.

An Indian burial ground at Suquamish, Wash., 14 miles from Seattle, contains the grave of the great chief. A granite shaft erected there by the people of Seattle is inscribed: "Seattle, Chief of the Suquamish and Allied tribes, died June 7, 1866, the firm friend of the Whites, and for him the City of Seattle was named by its founders." Each year the grave is the scene of a memorial ceremony conducted by local Boy Scouts on Scout Anniversary Day. In Seattle itself, a bronze statue represents the Indian leader in a typical pose, his hand outstretched in a gesture of perpetual peace and friendship.

SELOCTA (Creek) was a Creek chief.

SEQUAREESERE(Onondaga; fl. 18th century), was a chief of the Onondaga during the middle of the 18th century. He attended a treaty negotiation in Montreal in 1756 and a council meeting at Fort Johnson, New York in 1757. His name is included among those at a conference at Oswego in August 1759, and he signed a treaty at Fort Stanwix in 1768.

SEQUENE (Arawak; fl. 15th century), was chief of a group of Arawak Indians who, shortly before Columbus' arrival in the New World in 1492, sailed from their homeland in the Greater Antilles to Florida, where they settled the site known as Abaibo. Sequene's son, Carlos, was well-known to the Spanish.

SEQUIDONGQUEE (Seneca; fl. late 18th and early 19th centuries), also Little Beard signed the treaties of 1790, 1797, 1815, and 1826 on behalf of his tribe. Two Seneca chiefs, one the successor of the other, shared both the Indian and English names, and it is not always possible to know which chief signed which treaties. The first lived at Little Beard's town (Cuylerville), New York during the period of the American Revolution. The second was renowned as an orator.

SEQUOYAH (Cherokee; *c.* 1760– 1843), or Sequoya, Sikwayi, or Sogwali; English name George Guess, Guest, or Gist, invented a syllabary or alphabet for the Cherokee language in the early 19th century. He was born, possibly about 1760, in the Indian village, near Fort Loudon on the Tennessee River. Sequoyah's mother was Wurteh, sister of several Cherokee chiets; his father was a white man, probably Nathaniel Gist, a friend of George Washington.

Sequoyah grew up in northern Cherokee country during a period of warfare between the Cherokees and the white Americans which lasted until 1795. He later moved to Alabama in order to be further from the encroachments of whites.

Sequoyah joined a Cherokee regiment of the U.S. Army and served against the Creeks in 1813-1814. In 1816 he attended a conference at Turkeytown, which met with Andrew Jackson and ceded to the United States considerable Cherokee territory. In 1818 Sequoyah joined a group emigrating west to Arkansas, where a number of Cherokee had already settled.

Sequoyah was a hunter and fur trader, and later a farmer and mechanic. He also became a skilled silversmith and painter. Accident, disease, or war injury had made him lame, and this disability may have contributed to his interest in intellectual pursuits. By about 1809 he had become convinced that writing was a source of white power, which allowed greater accumulation of knowledge and transmission of information over longer distances than did speech alone and consequently believed it would greatly benefit his fellow tribesmen if they could read and write in their own language. Although Moravian and other missionaries had tried, they failed to construct an alphabet suitable to the Cherokee language, so that English was the only available language for written communication.

Other Cherokees ridiculed Sequoyah's efforts to produce a Cherokee alphabet. Some, believing him to be engaged in witchcraft, burned his house and records. But Sequoyah persisted for 12 years. At first he tried to create a symbol for each spoken word of his language, but eventually decided that this method would produce an unmanageably large number of characters. By 1821 he had perfected an alphabet of 86 symbols, each symbol but one representing a single syllable of the spoken language. The idea behind the syllabary was entirely independent of written English (Sequoyah never learned to speak, read, or write, although he used letters of the English alphabet as characters, giving them different sound values in Cherokee than they have in English. Other characters of the syllabary were Sequoyah's own inventions.

In 1821 Sequoyah returned to the eastern Cherokee homeland, where he held a public demonstration in which he and his young daughter showed how messages could be transmitted by writing. After he taught his system to a group of men and they also proved able to understand messages communicated solely by writing, Cherokee leaders became convinced of the value of his invention. Within a few years almost every Cherokee was literate in his own language.

Sequoyah then returned to Arkansas and taught his alphabet to the western Cherokees, thus allowing communication in writing between the eastern and western groups. Missionaries, realizing the advantages of his alphabet, began to translate religious tracts and educational materials into written Cherokee. In 1828 the *Cherokee Phoenix*, a weekly newspaper printed in both Cherokee and English, began publication. For his contribution, the Cherokee Nation awarded Sequoyah a medal and a pension.

After 1823 Sequoyah remained with the Arkansas Cherokees. In 1828 he was a member of a delegation of western Cherokee which traveled to Washington, D.C., to discuss the problems of white encroachment on Cherokee lands. The western Cherokees agreed to exchange their territory for a tract of land in what is now Oklahoma, and in 1829 Sequoyah moved to what is now Sequoyah County, Oklahoma. There he continued to farm, work his salt lick, and teach his alphabet. In 1839 he used his influence to promote peace between the western

Cherokees and the eastern Cherokee survivors of
the Trail of Tears, those who had been forced by the
U.S. Army to leave their homes in Georgia and
move to Indian Territory.

In his later years Sequoyah unsuccessfully attempted to construct a common grammar for various tribes. In 1842 he set out to search for a legendary tribe of lost Cherokees reputed to have moved
west in the distant past. He died in 1843 in the
mountains of Mexico during this journey. A memorial was erected in his honor in the U.S. Capitol. The
redwood trees of California, the Sequoias, were
named after him.

Sequoyah has long been cited as a great educator
of his people, who contributed to their advancement
and to the adoption of white civilization. An alternative interpretation of his life suggests instead
that Sequoyah was primarily a traditionalist who
sought to preserve Cherokee culture through the
use of his syllabary. Recently, a group of Sequoyah's
descendents have contested traditional accounts of
their ancestor's life, denying that Sequoyah invented the syllabary attributed to him, and maintaining that he was one of a long line of warrior-
scribes who used an alphabet that was centuries old
and that he was a·vigorous opponent of those
Cherokees who were willing to give up their own
culture and adopt that of whites.

SETANGYA (Kiowa; 1810– 1871), was noted
Kiowa chief and medicine-man, and leader of the
principal war society of the tribe. Commonly known
to the whites as Satank, he was born in the Black-
Hills region about 1810. His paternal grandmother
was a Sarsi. He became prominent at an early age,
and is credited with having been a principal agent
in negotiating the final peace between the Kiowa
and the Cheyenne about 1840. His name heads the
list of signers of the noted Medicine Lodge treaty of
1867. In 1870 his son was killed by the whites while
raiding in Texas. The father went down into Texas,

gathered the bones into a bundle, and brought them back. He carried them with him upon a special horse until he was killed about a year later. That year, he led an attack on a wagon train in Texas. Boasting of the deed, he was arrested by military authorties in Oklahoma and sent to Texas for trial. He refused, however, to be a prisoner and, instead, sang his own death song prior to being shot to death in an escape attempt.

SEWACKENAEM(Esopus; fl. 17th century), a chief of the Esopus, signed several treaties during the middle of the 17th century. The Esopus sachem attended the council of 1658, the peace treaty of 1660, signed a treaty with Governor Nicolls in 1665, was one of the five Esopus chiefs at the treaty of 1669, and renewed deeds in 1674 and 1681.

SEWID, JAMES (Kwakiutl; 1913–   ), the first elected chief of his tribe following the elimination of the system of hereditary chiefs, developed the inter-tribal council and established a committee to handle problems of juvenile delinquency. As a child, Sewid was taught great respect for tribal customs and traditions despite the fact that native culture was in a state of decline. At the age of 10 he began his career as a fisherman, a career that saw him rise to prominence in the Canadian salmon fishing industry. Torn between two worlds — the one of his Indian ancestors and the other of his European-descended Canadian contemporaries — Sewid agonized over what role traditional customs should play in modern Indian life. Finally, he struck a compromise, participating in Canadian political life and the Anglican Church while living in a Kwakiutl community. Selected by the National Film Board of Canada to portray himself in a film, *No Longer Vanishing*, Sewid also wrote his auto-biography *(Guest Never Leave Hungry*, Yale University Press, 1969) which describes his efforts and achievements as chief.

SHABBONA (Ottawa; fl. 19th century), sometimes spelled Shabonee, Chambly, Chabonne, Shab-eh-nay or Sho-bon-ier is remembered in Illinois as a prominent Ottawa chief in "The Three Fires" Confederacy. It consisted of Potawatomi, Chippewa, and Ottawa who resided north of Peoria on the Illinois River and throughout the northeastern part of the state. Several times he represented his group at treaty councils with the whites. He grew to be a staunch friend of the latter.

It cannot be determined exactly when or where he was born. But his birth probably occurred at the beginning of the American Revolution. Early in life he joined *The Three Fires* group and married at least one Potawatomi wife.

During the War of 1812, he took up arms against the Americans. Yet he switched his allegience at the conclusion of this conflict. Shabbona ruled as a village, or peace, chief of the Potawatomi, Ottawa, and Chippewa in Illinois. His name appears as a leader for the first time in a treaty negotiated at St. Louis on August 24, 1816. Nine years later, Thomas Forsyth (an Indian agent at Peoria) declared that Shabbona, an Ottawa, and White Dog, a Chippewa, acted as the principal chiefs of *The Three Fires* in his district. That same year, Shabbona participated in a treaty concluded at Prairie du Chien (August 19, 1825) as an Ottawa delegate. And the following month he drew rations and supplies at Fort Armstrong — on Rock Island — for his followers.

At this time his villages extended along the Spoon River, but in 1829 he complained to William Clark, Superintendent of Indian Affairs, that he had been threatened and driven from that location. His new settlement, called As-sim-in-eh-kon, lay in or near Paw Paw Grove, a wooded area now within Paw Paw Township of DeKalb County and Wyoming Township of Lee Country. Thus, the treaty of Prairie du Chien (July 29, 1829) reserved two sections of land at this site for his *use*.

When James M. Bucklin commenced surveying a route for the proposed Illinois and Michigan Canal in 1830, he found himself in need of an expert guide and engaged Shabbona for the task. A year later, the Chief still lived at Paw Paw Grove, although his reserve had not yet been surveyed and assigned to him. Many of the white settlers knew Shabbona since he often journeyed to Peoria or the Spoon River Valley to secure supplies or hunt. He also sought wild game along the Sangamon until the nervous inhabitants there complained of these excursions. So, Shabbona petitioned the President of the United States for protection. But after a meeting with William Clark at St. Louis in November of 1831, he finally agreed to confine his expeditions to northern Illinois.

With the coming of the Black Hawk War in 1832, Shabbona volunteered his expert services despite the fact that many of the whites had treated him shabbily. Militia officers at Chicago, however, refused his offer. Nevertheless, the Chief led his warriors to the Rock River in June and joined Gen. Henry Atkinson's forces. In all, ninety-five men from *The Three Fires* (including twenty chiefs) were mustered into service on June 22. One month later, they all received discharges except Shabbona, Billy Caldwell, Waubonsee, and Perish Le Clair. These four leaders rendered outstanding service to the army as guides, spies, and messengers.

On October 20, 1832, another treaty was signed with the *Prairie* and *Kankakee* bands of Potawatomi, and Shabbona's two sections of land were again mentioned as being *reserved* for him. In addition, he received forty dollars for a horse which had been stolen from him during the war.

By the treaty of Chicago, September 26 and 27, 1833, *The Three Fires* gave up all their lands around Lake Michigan; Shabbona also witnessed this cession of land to the United States. One article stipulated that the faithful Chief's two sections of land were now granted "in fee simple to him, his heirs and assigns forever." Because of his patriotic service in the Black Hawk War, he received in addition, a yearly pension of $200 for life. He had ridden countless hours in the saddle to warn frontiersmen of Black Hawk's approach with a Sauk and Fox war party.

From 1835 until 1838, many members of *The Three Fires* were officially escorted west of the Mississippi. Shabbona seems to have traveled with them, but later he returned to Paw Paw Grove. In 1838 he begged the government to survey his reserve. When Washington officials appeared reluctant to permit an Indian to own land, Shabbona asked them in 1839 to buy back his grant. Perhaps this forthright request hastened the survey. G. M. Butler laid out the reserve of 1,280 acres in December of 1842; it included all of Section 23, half of Section 25, and half of Section 26 in Township 38 North, Range 3 East of the 3rd Principal Meridian, an area just north of Shabbona Grove in Shabbona Township of DeKalb County and not at Paw Paw Grove as the treaty had specified.

Since the old Chief often wandered about the country, squatters soon invaded his preserve, and the grant went up for sale on July 21, 1849. Before the buyers could obtain clear titles, however, the United States government was forced to appropriate $1,600 and purchase the tract from Shabbona in 1852.

According to a letter written at Shabbona Grove on July 1, 1854, this reknowned Chief then resided west of the Mississippi with remnants of his band and had been there for two or three years. Not until about 1855 did he go back to Ottawa, Illinois. There, friends purchased a parcel of land for him on June 27, 1857. It consisted of twenty acres in the East Half of the Southeast Fractional Quarter of Section 20, Township 33 North, Range 6 East of the 3rd P. M.: a spot on the south bank of the Illonois River between Morris and Seneca in Morman Township of Grundy County. Upon this site, Shabbona constructed a simple lodge and pursued a quiet life. But when Lincoln and Douglas debated at Ottawa on August 21, 1858, Perry A. Armstrong, county clerk and close friend of the Chief, brought Shabbona to witness the historic event. In tribute to this Indian's standing in the community, officials accorded him a position of honor on the platform itself.

Shabbona remained active until the very day of his death, July 18, 1859. On the previous day, he had gotten wet and overexerted himself while out hunting. He died in his lodge, and the funeral took place at Morris the following day with burial being made in Evergreen Cemetry. His wife, Pokanoka, drowned in Mazon River on November 30, 1864, and was interred beside him.

A gray boulder — weighing several tons — stands over their graves. This munument has been there since October 23, 1903. It bears the single word "Shabbona" and carries the dates 1775-1859, although the year of his birth is not known for certain. Descendants of the well-known Chief visited his grave in 1949 and observed memorial services conducted by the Grundy County Historical Society. As long as people read the history of Illinois, the bravery and devotion of this Ottawa chief will not be forgotten.

SHAVEHEAD (Potawatomi; fl. 19th century), was an early 19th century Potawatomi chief who lived in southwestern Michigan and who was known for his hostility toward whites. Although his birth and death dates are uncertain, it is known that he participated in the Indian hostilities in the Great Lakes region that were finally culminated in the Indian participation in the War of 1812. A firm supporter of Tecumseh's Indian confederacy, Shavehead served under Topenebee, whose niece was Shavehead's wife, throughout the encounters of 1812 and 1813. He played a prominent part in the Fort Dearborn massacre of August 15, 1812, and participated in the Battle of the Thames in 1813.

The ferocity of the deeds he committed against whites gained for him the fear of both whites and fellow Indians, and led to the recitation of a number of tales, true and otherwise, concerning his bloody career. His death, like his deeds, is clouded with uncertain information. One story suggests he was killed by a survivor of Fort Dearborn, and another by a white hunter he encountered in the forest and immediately insulted and challenged.

SHAHWUNDAIS, (Chippewa; 1796– *c.* 1855),also John Sunday was converted to Methodism as a young man and devoted the remainder of his life to preaching and proselytizing among his people. Converted at a camp-meeting in 1826-27, Sunday immediately pursued a career as a Methodist minister. He learned to read and write and, following his ordination, assumed an active role in missionary work among the Chippewa.

Traveling as far as Lake Superior, Sunday helped establish permanent missions during the 1830s at Keweenaw Bay and at Ottawa Lake — both in Michigan. He was a tremendously effective preacher, and at Sault Ste Marie women were said to have forded streams with children in their arms just for the opportunity to hear him speak. Later in the 1830s he traveled throughout the United States, raising money for the Methodist missions in Canada.

Although Sunday's eloquence astonished those in attendance at the general council of the Christian Chippewa and Ottawa held at Saugeen, Ontario in 1845, no record of his activities exists after that date. Nevertheless, Sunday is believed to have lived until at least 1855.

SHEHEKE (Mandan; fl. 19th century), was a Mandan chief who entered the pages of recorded history when Meriweather Lewis and William Clark wintered at Fort Mandan in 1804-05. The fair-skinned Indian, also called Big White, was one of the first visitors. He was accompanied by his wife in whose arms was their baby. On her back was 100 pounds of meat for the explorers.

On the way back from the Pacific Coast in August 1806, Lewis and Clark stopped to visit their Mandan friends — and to invite one of the chiefs to return with them to greet the Great Father in Washington. Government officials were hopeful of impressing Indian guests with the might and wealth of white civilization. The chiefs, however, were reluctant to go. Finally, Sheheke volunteered, provided he could take his wife and child.

The chief was warmly received by President Thomas Jefferson in Washington, where he attended a dinner honoring the explores. Returning the Mandans to their home proved to be a long and costly process. The first attempt was made in the summer of 1807, but the small escort party, under Ensign Nathaniel Pryor, was forced by hostile Arkaras to return to St. Louis. In the second attempt a St. Louis Missouri Fur Company expedition, led by Auguste Pierre Chouteau, deposited the visitors at their village of Sept. 24, 1809.

Some say that Sheheke was welcomed with frantic joy; others, that the Mandans refused to believe his fantastic tales of life in Washington, Philadelphia, and St. Louis. Furthermore, only the coup stick entitled an Indian chief to glory in the eyes of his tribesmen. Perhaps the latter view accounts for Sheheke's second visit to St. Louis in 1812. Supposedly he was killed either by the Gros Ventres while returning to Mandan country or by the Sioux in a tribal fight.

SHICKSHACK (Winnebago; fl. 19th century), was a Winnebago chief, born in Wisconsin, who was a friend of the white settlers in the Great Lakes region. The Winnebago were involved in numerous confrontations with their traditional enemies the Chippewa. Shickshack was by nature a peaceful and jovial man, and could not participate in the constant feuding. In 1819 he and his people moved to the area of present Sangamon County, Illinois to avoid any further Winnebago-Chippewa hostilities. By 1820 his tribe numbered some 40 families inhabiting a village about 25 miles above the mouth of the Sangamon River. Shickshack's relations with the neighboring white settlers were always peaceful and amicable. Shickshack firmly bebieved in the necessity to maintain cooperation and peace with whites and also among the various Indian nations.

Because of these convictions, he would take no part in the differences between Black Hawk and Keokuk, nor in Black Hawk's ideas and actions that finally led to war. In 1827 he and his tribe removed themselves to northern Illinois once more in an attempt to avoid hostilities. Shickshack deplored the fighting initiated by Black Hawk in 1832. Although he did not participate in the war, he assisted in capturing Black Hawk after the defeat at the Bad Axe River, and in surrendering him to the U.S. forces. Shickshack attended the treaty negotiations ending the fighting.

In 1837 the Winnebago of Wisconsin entered into a treaty with the U.S. government that established the conditions for removal west. Although Shickshack did not participate in these negotiations, in 1839 he and his tribe joined the Winnebago nation in moving west of the Missisippi River to the present Kansas area, where he died some years later.

SHIKELLAMY (Oneida; ?— 1748), an Oneida chiefton, was the exponent of the colonial policy of the great federal Iroquois council at Onondaga, and was sent by it to the forks of the Susquehanna in 1728 to conserve the interests of the Six Nations and to keep watch over the Shawnee and Delaware Indians. He was a man of great dignity, and at all times showed marked kindness, especially to the missionaries. In the execution of his trust Shikellamy conducted many important embassies between the government of Pennsylvania and the Iroquois council at Onondaga, and he also attended many if not most of the councils held at Philadelphia, Conestoga, and elsewhere in the performance of his duties.

The importance of his office is evident from the fact that the valley of the Susquehanna, after the Conestoga were subjugated in 1676 by the Iroquois, was assigned by the Five Nations of Iroquois as a hunting ground to the Shawnee, Delawares, Conoy, Nanticoke, Munsee, Tutelo, Saponi, and Conestoga tribes. When the Mohawk sold the Wyoming region in Pennsylvania to the Susquehanna Land Co., although this tribe had never aided in the conquests made in this valley, the council at Onondaga began to realize that this section, with its valuable land and many dependent tribes, was worthy of careful attention; hence these tribes were made to understand that in the future they must transact all business with the propriety government solely through their deputy. With his residence fixed at Shamokin (now Sunbury), Pa., Shikellamy was promoted in 1745 to the full vicegerency over the tributary tribes in the Susquehanna valley, and intricate and important interests committed to him received the care of an astute statesman and diplomat.

The effects of the liquor traffic on the Indians led to prohibitory decrees on the part of the government of Pennsylvania, and later, evidently through the influence of traders, when these prohibitory measures became lax, Skikellamy in 1731 delivered an ultimatum to the Pennsylvania government that unless the liquor trade is better regulated, friendly relations between the proprietary government and the Six Nations would cease.

As the difficulties arising from the sale of liquor had forced a large number of Shawnee to migrate from the Susquehanna to the Ohio River in 1730, and as French emissaries were taking advantage of this condition to alienate the Shawnee from the

English interest, the governor decided in 1731 to send Shikellamy, "a trusty, good man, and a great lover of the English," to Onondaga to invite the Six Nations to Philadelphia.

In 1736 Shikellamy's influence was enlisted to bring about a conference at which the entire confederation of the Six Nations would be represented, and in less than two months' time Conrad Weiser informed the Governor of Pennsylvania that more than a hundred chiefs of the Iroquois with their retinues were on their way to Phildelphia. By this treaty of 1736 the Six Nations deeded all their Susquehanna lands south and east of the Blue Mountains. Some weeks later, when nearly all the leading Indians had departed, another deed was prepared and signed by the remaining Indians, which purported to include the lands ostensibly claimed by the Six Nations within the drainage of Delaware River south of the Blue Mountains — a treaty that, "established a precedent for an Iroquois claim to lands owned by the Delaware Indians," a claim that had never been advanced before. Weiser helped Shikellamy sow the seed which drenched Pennsylvania in blood from 1755 to 1764. In a war with the Delaware, Weiser had many good reasons for regarding Shikellamy as the key to the secret policies of the council of the Iroquois at Onondaga. In 1745 Shikellamy was requested by Governor Thomas to visit the Six Nations and gain peace with the Catawba.

The acquisition of firearms became a necessity to the Indian hunters and warriors. Shikellamy persuaded the colonial government to establish a forge at Shamokin. This was granted on condition that the Indians would permit the Moravians to begin a mission at the place, which the missionaries regarded as the greatest stronghold of paganism. To this proposal Shikellamy readily consented, and in April, 1747, a smithy and a mission house were erected there. A year later, Zeisberger, who had become proficient in the Mohawk tongue, became an assistant missionary at Shamokin, and while there began the preparation of an Onondaga dictionary under the interested instruction of Shikellamy. During this year (1748) Shikellamy received from Count Zinzendorf a silver knife, fork, and spoon, and an ivory drinking cup richly mounted in silver, accompanied with a message entreating him to hold fast to the gospel which he had heard from the count's own lips. This resulted in the conversion of Shikellamy at Bethlehem shortly afterward; he was not baptized by the Moravians, however, because he had been baptized many years before by a Jesuit priest in Canada. On his way to Shamokin he fell ill at Tulpehocking. Zeisberger, who had returned to his post, ministered to the stricken chieftain until his death. The colonial government sent a message of condolence, and requested the eldest son of Shikellamy, John or Thachnechtoris (Tagheghdoarus) to serve as the Iroquois deputy governor until the council at Onondage could make a permanent appointment.

SHINGABAWASSIN (Chippewa; 1763–? 1837), was a Chippewa chief prominent during the first quarter of the 19th century. He was the eldest son of Maidosagee, the son of Gitcheojeedebun. His residence, during most of his years at least, was on the banks of St. Mary's River, Michigan, at the outlet of Lake Superior. His life, so far as known, was characterized by but few marked incidents, largely spent in behalf of the welfare of his people. During his younger days he took an active part in the war expeditions of his band, especially those against the Sioux, but after assuming the responsibilities of his official life he became a strong advocate of peace. At the councils convened for the purpose of entering into treaties, especially those at Prairie du Chien in 1825, Fond du Lac in 1826, and Butte des Mortes in 1827, he was the leading speaker and usually the most important person among the Indian delegates. He seems to have risen, to a large extent, above the beliefs of his people, and even went so far in one of the councils as to advise making known to the whites the situation of the great copper deposits, although these were regarded by the Indians as sacred. A favorite scheme which he advanced and vigorously advocated, but without effect, was to have the United States set apart a special reservation for the "half-breeds." In addition to the treaties mentioned Shingabawassin signed the treaty of Sault Ste Marie, June 11, 1820. He died between 1828 and 1837, and was succeeded as chief by his son Kabay Noden.

SHORT BULL (Brulé Sioux; *c.* 1845—?) came into prominence in 1890 when he was chosen to be a member of the Sioux delegation to visit Wovoka, the Indian "Messiah," at Pyramid Lake, Nevada. On his return he represented himself as the special vicar of Wovoka, and later, after having been imprisoned by the Federal authorities, claimed to be the "Messiah" himself. He gained great popularity with the Sioux during the "Ghost Dance" craze, but with the abatement of the excitement his popularity waned and he fell into disrepute.

SILVERHEELS, JAY (Mohawk; *c.* 1920–),became famous as "Tonto" in the Lone Ranger television series. He was born Harry Smith around 1920. Silverheels began playing Tonto in 1949. He also acted in the film *The Lone Ranger* (1955) and a number of other films — including *The Prairie* (1947), *Broken Arrow* (1950), and *War Arrow* (1953).

SILOCTA (Creek; fl. 1825), was a Creek chief who flourished around 1825. His name is also spelled Selocta. Taking the side of the U.S. in the War of 1812, he fought bravely with Andrew Jackson's troops. He opposed removal to Indian territory, appealing to Jackson to use his influence to preserve the land west of the Coosa River for Creeks.

SINNONQUIRESSE (Mohawk; fl. late 17th and early 18th centuries), a Mohawk chief, represented the tribe on several occasions to the colonial government at Albany, New York. Sinnonquiresse spoke at Albany in 1691, 1696, 1700, 1701, and 1702. He signed the Beaver land treaty in 1701.

SINTE GLESKA (Dakota; *c.* 1823–?   ), or Spotted Tail was a member of the Sichangu Tribe of the Dakota Nation. As a young man living in the Platte River region of Western Nebraska, Sinte Gleska distinguished himself as an excellent hunter and warrior, thus gaining his peoples support as head chief. Sinte Gleska was of sharp wit and used both his virility and rationale in attaining results. In 1855 Sinte Gleska was taken to Ft. Leavenworth, Kansas as a prisoner. During this journey east he soon realized the old way of living for the Dakota was doomed and that to fight with the whites, the Dakota might be able to win a battle, but would never be able to win an all out war. When the Dakota were placed on reservations, he alone knew that his people must change their life style, but he also knew that this change must come about slowly. He partially achieved this goal by using his great ability in persuading the government officials that his way was right.

He used excellent diplomacy constantly when discussing important matters with the government. He prevented the government from relocating the Dakota Nation to Indian territory (Oklahoma). He kept the whiskey traders out of the reservation. He kept his own people from mounting war parties on the whites, which would surely be reason for removal to Indian Territory. When several members of this tribe did kill a white man, he made them surrender themselves to the government, then hired a lawyer for them whom he paid out of his own pocket.

Sinte Gleska was a large man with strikingly handsome features. Although he didn't have an education in the white man tradition, he was very intelligent and learned from every experience he encountered.

Born during the winter of 1823–24 on the White River of South Dakota in the vicinity of where the Big White Clay Creek empties into it, Sinte Gleska was given the boyhood name of Jumping Buffalo. His father was Tangle Hair and his mother, Walks With Pipe. By 1832 the Sichangu had migrated to the North Platte River Region. During his younger years in this area, Jumping Buffalo acquired his adult name Sinte Gleska (being named after a racoon tail). Later he acquired many *apa honor's* (coups) while fighting enemy Indian Tribes and white soldiers. During his lifetime Sinte Gleska earned 26 *apa honors.*

In 1851 Sinte Gleska, an established war leader, was at the signing of the Ft. Laramie Treaty. This treaty was the beginning of boundary limitations for the Dakota.

In 1854 Sinte Gleska led his warriors in the killing of Lieutenant Gratton and his men. In retaliation, General Harvey surprised the unsuspecting Sichangu and defeated them in 1855. Sinte Gleska was wounded and taken prisoner and sent to the military prison in Ft. Leavenworth, Kansas. It was during this time that Sinte Gleska got a glimpse of the nation called the United States. Upon returning from prison in 1856, Sinte Gleska was determined in keeping out of trouble with the white man. But Indian killers among the Colorado volunteers brought on a general state of war. In 1864 the prairie became alive with Indians seeking revenge for the slaughter of Indian men, women, and children. By 1865, Sinte Gleska could no longer restrain his men, so he led them in the attack and destruction of Julesburg, Colorado.

The winter of 1865–66 Sinte Gleska became known as the Head Chief of the Sichangu.

The Ft. Laramie Treaty of 1868 established the Great Dakota Reservation. Sinte Gleska signed the treaty but was stunned when he learned that their new agency was moved from the Platte River to the Missouri in South Dakota. The Sichangu needing supplies and wanting to trade, had to move to the Missouri Area.

Sinte Gleska won the approval of many Government officials in 1870 when he went to Washington, D.C. to visit. Then in 1871–72 he was selected to take the Grand Duke Alexis of Russia on a Buffalo Hunting Trip, Dakota style. As a result of this and through other negotiations, Sinte Gleska was allowed to move his agency west of the Missouri in 1873. From 1873 to 1875, Sinte Gleska used every means available to him in keeping his beloved people from fighting with the whites. He also informed his own police force to keep the whiskey runners off the reservation.

Gold was discovered in the Great Lakota Reservation at a place called the Black Hills. With settlers and gold seekers flooding into the reservation, the government decided to try and buy or lease the land from the Dakota. Sinte Gleska offered a sensible request for mining rights at $400,000.00 a year. But the Dakota Nation refused to lease or sell the Black Hills.

As a result of this refusal to sell the Black Hills, the government declared all Dakota outside the reservation hostile and sent the Army after them. In 1876 the Dakota defeated General Crook on the Rosebud River and General Custer on the Little Big Horn River. These defeats caused the Army to build up its strength against the Dakota and created government policy to remove all Dakota to Indian Territory. Sinte Gleska disapproved of this removal plot and continually spoke out against it until the policy was dismissed. In 1877 Sinte Gleska was successful in persuading several Dakota groups into returning to the Reservation. By 1879 Sinte Gleska was overwhelmed with the problems of transforming 10,000 Dakota from buffalo hunters into life on the reservation.

During this reservation period opposition to Sinte Gleska developed. Complaints stated that Sinte Gleska was secretly collecting grazing fees from cattlemen, on the reservation and pocketing the money for his own use, that he sold Dakota lands to the railroads, that he was running the government police to suit himself, and that he was a non-progressive. A member of the government police force by the name of Crow Dog posed as the champion of the common people against this said tyrant, Sinte Gleska. But Sinte Gleska in a speech before the Tribal Council exonerated himself of all accusations. Following the speech the council voted to retain Sinte Glesca as head chief. The opposition party began to dwindle in numbers and Crow Dog became bitter. On August 5, 1881, while riding his horse home from a tribal council meeting, Sinte Gleska was shot and killed by Crow Dog. The killing took place approximately one mile east of present day Rosebud, South Dakota.

General Cook states that he believes Crow Dog had been instigated to kill Sinte Gleska by Black Crow, a headman of the Sichangu (Brulé) whose ambition was to oust Sinte Gleska and gain the Chieftainship.

Another story as to the reason for the murder of Sinte Gleska is that Sinte Gleska stole the wife of Medicine Bear. Crow Dog, the champion of the common people, then took up the cause of Medicine Bear and shot Sinte Gleska for not returning her.

Henry Lelar, Chief Clerk at Rosebud knew the Sichangu very well. He states that Crow Dog deliberately planned the killing with the hope of succeeding Sinte Gleska as head chief.

No matter which of the above stories you choose to believe, the fact remains that the killing of Sinte Gleska ended the history of the Sichangu as a tribal entity. The Government would not recognize another head chief and began planning for the destruction of authority of the minor chiefs.

Sinte Gleska considered by many to be the greatest Sichangu leader that lived, lies buried on the hill just north of Rosebud Agency in South Dakota.

SITTING BULL (Hunkpapa; 1831– December 15, 1890), was the Hunkpapa Sioux chief whose name stands as a symbol for the distrust of the Indian for the white man and for determination to resist white domination.

Until the 1860s Sitting Bull had managed to remain aloof from white men pressing insistantly into his beloved country. He wanted no part of their treaties, their lies, or their handouts. His chief concerns were hunting, Indian-enemy warfare, and the usual domestic problems of a family man. (He is said to have had nine wives, not counting Catherine Weldon, thought by some to be his white squaw.) Then, in the summer of 1863, his hunting party was involved in a skirmish with Gen. Alfred Sulley's troops in the Battle of Killdeer Mountain. Sitting Bull took to the warpath, although he never attacked white settlements. About 1867 he became head chief of the entire Sioux nation.

Late in 1875 the commissioner of Indian Affairs ordered all Sioux onto reservations by Jan. 31, 1876 or be deemed hostile. Sitting Bull had heard that many Indians who had accepted agency life were half-starved. Even had he wished to obey the command, the winter was to severe to march his people 240 miles to the nearest agency. He was therefore considered hostile, as were thousands of other Indians who flocked, early in the summer, to his camp in the valley of the Little Big Horn River in Montana Territory.

Sitting Bull was a missionary and a prophet. On June 14 he performed the torturesome sun dance wherein he saw soldiers falling into his camp. His vision was fulfilled 11 days later when the U.S. 7th Cavalry attacked the village. Lt. Col. George A. Custer and the men under his immediate command were destroyed in the Battle of the Little Big Horn.

Sitting Bull

A shocked nation demanded that the government end the Indian threat forever. Col. Nelson A. Miles was ordered to Dakota Territory where, in October, under a flag of truce, he and Sitting Bull talked of peace. Supposedly he told the General, God Almighty made me an Indian but not an agency Indian, and I do not intend to become one.

Lack of game, plus military pursuit, combined to drive sitting Bull into Canada in 1877. His plea to Dominion authorities to provide a reservation was refused on the grounds that the refugees already had a reservation in their own country. Faced again with starvation, this last remnant of the once great Sioux nation was forced to surrender at Fort Buford, N.D., in 1881. Before he was permitted to rejoin his people at the Standing Rock agency, 1883, he was detained as a prisoner of war at Fort Randall. Considered troublesome by Indian agent Maj. James McLaughlin, Sitting Bull was often farmed out for exhibition purposes. He spent the summer of 1885 with Buffalo Bill's Wild West show.

For six years Sitting Bull fought to preserve for his people the 11 million acres of land guaranteed by treaty, but in 1889 he met total defeat. As tools of Major McLaughlin's government-appointed Indian chiefs secretly signed away their birthright to become wards of the government, drought, near-famine, and disease followed. Out of despair his remaining followers embraced the Ghost Dance cult, spread by a Nevada Piaute named Wovoka. Sitting Bull neither endorsed nor denounced this craze, but since dancing went on daily in his camp, he stood accused as an agitator. Many settlers, fearing another Indian outbreak, fled the country.

Major McLaughlin claimed that he could prevent bloodshed by having Sitting Bull arrested by reservation Indian police. Before dawn on Dec. 15, 1890, more than 40 policemen, some of them relatives of Sitting Bull, descended upon his camp. They dragged the sleeping man from his bed and tried to put him on his horse. At first, the proud chief did not resist, but as his captors' rough treatment increased, he became angry and shouted, "I am not going. Take action." Two policemen fired into his body, but Red Tomahawk, who fired from behind, claimed credit for the murder. Eight of the chiefs followers, including his 17-year-old son, and six Indian police were killed in the general melee.

Sitting Bull was buried in the post cemetery at Fort Yates, N.D. Many years later his remains were taken to Mobridge, S.D., where a granite shaft marks the final resting place of a great Sioux chief.

SKANAHWAHTI (Onondaga; fl. 19th century), also John Buck, firekeeper of the Canadian Onondaga, assisted Horatio Hale in preparing *The Iroquois Book of Rites* in 1883. As the official keeper and interpreter of the tribal wampum, Skanahwahti was greatly admired. He died at Brantford around 1893.

SKANDAWTI (Onondaga; fl. 17th century), an Onondaga chief, killed himself when his honor was defiled. In October 1647, Skandawti led a procession to the Hurons, returning fifteen Huron prisoners and offering seven great belts. The Hurons sent a return party early in 1648, but they kept Skandawti as a hostage. When the Huron party was destroyed by Mohawks, the Onondaga chief considered the attack to be a blight upon his own honor and killed himself.

SKENANDOA (Oneida; *c.* 1704– March 11, 1816), also spelled Schenandoah, Shenondoa, Scanondo, and Skennondon, was a principal Oneida chief in New York, and a friend of the white colonists. During the American Revolution he espoused the cause of Iroquois confederacy neutrality but often gave assistance to the U.S. He aided the Boston colonists at the outbreak of hostilities, helped prevent invasions from Canada, prevented the destruction of the

German Flats, New York settlements, and provided scouts and spies to the colonies.

In May, 1775 he led 11 other Oneida chiefs in officially declaring their neutrality. In September, 1776 he refused to participate in the Niagara council ending Iroquois neutrality, and was joined by a number of Tuscarora chiefs. The Oneida and Tuscarora were considered "dissenting bodies" by the other Iroquois nations, and toward the end of the Revolution Skenandoa had to take refuge at Schenectady· from the British and pro-British Indians who, under Gen. John Burgoyne, attacked the main Oneida village.

In 1794 Skenandoa pledged continued neutrality during the Iroquois uprisings. He protested but permitted recruiting of Indian volunteers during the War of 1812. To him the conflict was the confrontation between Tecumseh's teachings and the teachings of Christianity.

When first introduced to the Iroquois nations, alcohol was taken usually during celebrations, but like many chiefs of his day Skenandoa became a chronic problem drinker. While in Albany in 1775 he became so drunk that his badge of chieftainship was stolen from him. He pledged never to drink again, and through the Rev. Samuel Kirkland, missionary to the Oneida, became a devout Christian. After the Revolution the economic and social situation of the Indians declined rapidly. By 1812 Skenandoa resumed drinking. He died at Oneida Castle, New York.

SLEEPING WOLF (Kiowa; *c.* 1840–1877), after serving as a representative of his people to Washington in 1872, returned to lead the Kiowa in a bloody uprising during 1874–75. Sleeping Wolf is a hereditary name among the Kiowa; the first Sleeping Wolf negotiated a peace treaty with the Comanche around the year 1790. During 1874–75, the Kiowa—in alliance with the Comanche, Cheyenne, and Kiowa Apache—attempted to break out of their reservation. The Sleeping Wolf who was one of the leaders of this revolt was killed in 1877 while quarreling with a fellow Kiowa tribesman.

SMITH, DON LELOOSKA (Cherokee; August 31, 1933–   ), has distinguished himself as a wood-carver, lecturer, and dance programmer. His woodcarvings follow the styles and traditions of the Northwest Coast tribes, but in addition to woodcarving Smith is an authority on Indian dance, drama, music, and other forms of arts and crafts. In 1966 he received an award from the Inter-Tribal Indian Ceremonial in Gallup, New Mexico. Presently, Smith lives in Ariel, Washington and is affiliated with the Oregon Museum of Science and Industry.

SMITH, FINIS (Cherokee; 20th century), a Cherokee Indian, was the founder of the militant Five County Cherokee Movement in 1966. The movement was formed to protect and defend the Indians' fishing and hunting rights. The issue was precipitated by the arrest of a Cherokee for hunting, despite U.S. treaties with the Cherokees guaranteeing hunting rights. Smith's participation was valuable because he was an older man and a religious leader, and thus could not be dismissed as an impulsive youth.

SMITH, KEELY (Cherokee; 1935–   ), achieved fame as a popular singer, recording artist, and actress. She was born in 1935. In her twenties she made a number of records and appeared on national television variety shows. Keely Smith has received numerous awards as a performer, including a Grammy (1958). She is a member of the American Indian Center of Los Angeles.

SMITH, NIMROD JARRETT (Cherokee; c. 1838–1893), was an eastern Cherokee chief whose followers were among the few who refused to move west of the Mississippi. Known to his people as *Tsalaiihi*, he is remembered as a defender of the rights of the tiny band of Cherokees who remained in their ancestral home.

As a young man Smith enlisted in the Confederate army. At the close of the war he held the rank of sergeant of his all Indian company. Ten years after his return to the Cherokee reservation in North Carolina he was chosen chief of his tribe. His entire chieftainship was spent defending and clarifying the rights of his people. It was under his auspices that the first schools were established for the eastern Cherokees. Also his efforts solidified claims made by the Cherokees upon their lands in North Carolina.

SMOHALLA (Wanapum or Sokulk; *c.* 1818—1907), founder of the Dreamer religion, typified the 19th century Indian prophet in that he preached a doctrine that called for a return to primitive ways and unremitting hostility to white culture. After distinguishing himself as a warrior, Smohalla turned preacher and medicine man, achieving a degree of prominence during the 1850s. His fame prompted a jealous neighboring chief to provoke a fight which nearly resulted in Smohalla's death. But the medicine man, left for dead, managed to make his way to the Columbia River. He floated downstream in a boat, and eventually set out wandering along the Pacific coast. Smohalla traveled all the way down to Mexico and then back up through Arizona, Utah, Nevada—finally reaching his home in Washington. His tribe, of course, thought he had been resurrected from the dead and from then on considered him to be a miracle worker.

Smohalla seized upon the opportunity, and—blessed with a fine capacity for oratory—claimed that he had been to the spirit world where he had been given a message for all Indians. Stay away from the reservations, he counseled. Cling to the ancient tribal traditions, he told his followers, and the gods would respond favorably. They would send back other Indians from the dead to drive out the white invaders. A golden age for all tribes would follow their adoption of this atavistic religion.

The Dreamer cult combined Roman Catholic ritual, military parades, Mormon practices, and ancient Indian customs; but it depended especially upon bells, drums, and a rhythmic dance to produce an hypnotic and hallucinatory effect upon its adherents. The object of all this was to communicate with the gods who would then help the oppressed Indians throw off all vestiges of white culture. Like most of the messianic movements of the 19th century, however, Smohalla's religion was an outgrowth of defeat—a weird offshoot that took root in the fertile seedbed of desperation.

The white conquest of aboriginal life in North America was all but complete by the time (1872) Smohalla acquired a substantial following. Landless, regulated by government agents on a circumscribed reservation, the North American natives clutched eagerly at the optimistic vision Smohalla inspired. One of the most remarkable effects of the cult on the course of civil affairs was the resistance of Chief Joseph and his Nez Perce band to the government's notice that the Indians had to vacate the Wallowa Valley in Oregon. Eventually, however, Indian resistance crumbled, and Smohalla died—distraught at the dwindling number of his disciples—in 1907.

SNEED, WOODROW (Cherokee; 20th century), is a Cherokee Indian, attorney and government official who was born on a reservation in North Carolina. Sneed received his law degree from Harvard University. In the course of his varied career, he has been deputy director of the Community Action Program on a Navajo Reservation and has received two academic appointments. He was named a White House Fellow in 1969.

SOIONES (Onondaga; fl. 17th century), although a Huron by birth, was a naturalized Onondaga who led his adopted people in warfare against—and ultimate conquest of—the Hurons. A prominent Onondaga chief in the embassy to the Hurons in 1647, Soiones helped destroy the Huron tribes in 1648 and 1649, ending an age-old conflict and assuring the supremacy of the Iroquois Confederacy.

SOULIGNY (Menominee; 1785–1864), a war chief of the Menominee, joined Tecumseh in an alliance with the British against the United States during the War of 1812. Grandson of a French trader and a Menominee woman, Souligny played a prominent role in the capture of Fort Mackinaw from its American defenders in 1812. The next year, he and about 50 Menominee warriors fought with Tecumseh at the battle of Fort Meigs in Ohio.

Unlike Tecumseh, though, Souligny survived the War of 1812, and by the 1830s his animosities toward the Americans had diminished considerably. With the outbreak of the Black Hawk War in 1832, Souligny sided with the United States and refused to aid the beleaguered chief of the Sauk and Fox Indians. Although stout and without one eye, Souligny was reputed to be a handsome chief. At the age of 70 he could still speak with great vigor; during a visit to the editor of the *Milwaukee Sentinel* in 1855, he made an eloquent plea for the return of an Indian child kidnapped by white people.

SPEMICALAWBA (Shawnee; fl. 19th century), also spelled Spamagelabe and better known among whites as Capt. James Logan, was a Shawnee chief born late in the 18th century who loyally served the United States in the War of 1812 even though his mother was Tecumseh's sister. As a young boy Spemicalawba was captured (1786) by Benjamin Logan who was leading a miltary expedition against the Ohio tribes. Logan raised the boy, sent him through school, gave him his own name, and finally allowed him to return to his tribe in Wapakoneta, Ohio. By this time Spemicalawba was a steadfast, good humored, but fiercly loyal friend of the Americans.

After attempting to discourage Tecumseh from his intentions of fighting alongside the British, Spemicalawba enlisted as James Logan in the American army to serve as a scout and spy in the Ohio region during the War of 1812. At the onset of hostilities, after the fall of Fort Dearborn (Chicago) and Detroit, Logan worked from Fort Wayne, Indiana Territory. He served under Gen. James Winchester, commander of the Army of the Northwest, in a campaign to destroy the corn crops in the Maumee River area. Logan and two other Indians proceeded along the Maumee well in advance of Winchester. Encountering a British captain accompanied by five Indians, Logan and his comrades were taken prisoner, but at the right moment they attacked their captors, and killed the captain and two of his men. Badly wounded from a gun shot, Logan made his way back to Winchester's encampment where he died November 22, 1812 and was buried with full military honors befitting a captain. Winchester's campaign fell apart shortly thereafter from an outbreak of typhus. Logansport, Indiana is named after Spemicalawba.

SPOTTED ARM (Winnebago; *c.* 1722–? *c.* 1835), was held as a hostage during the Black Hawk War of 1832, and later was removed with his followers to the west side of Mississippi River. He derived his name from his habit of painting an old war wound to make it appear as though his arm was freshly wounded. Held hostage in 1832 to assure the good behavior of the Winnebago during Black Hawk's War, Spotted Arm later was ordered to move his people west of the Mississippi. This influential Winnebago chief died a few years following the removal.

SPRING, MAY R. (Tonawanda; May 17, 1899–   ), has served the Tonawanda Indians as a community worker. Employed at one time by the New York State Department of Social Welfare, May R. Spring's primary affiliation as a community worker has been with the Tonawanda Community House in Akron, New York; this affiliation has also included tenure as president, secretary, and member of the board of directors. Spring has also been active in the Tonawanda Indian Baptist Church.

SQUANDO (Abnaki; fl. 17th century), was a 17th century Abnaki sachem of the Sokoki people of the Saco River region. Known as the *sagamore of Saco*, Squando was described by Increase Mather as a "strange, enthusiastical sagamore."

Squando claimed to have had visions in which God appeared and told him to observe the sabbath, to avoid liquor, to pray, and to listen to the word preached. All this Squando did for several years. A vision also told him that God had left the English people to be destroyed by the Indians.

It us said that about 1675 some drunken English sailors, either to achieve mischief or to test a report that Indian children could swim instinctively from birth, overturned a canoe containing Squando's wife and child. Although the mother managed to swim with the child to safety, the child died a few days later. Anger over this incident (and probably also over the increasing white encroachment on Indian lands and the kidnapping and sale of Indians into slavery) led Squando to join in the war against the English in 1675.

Squando took part in the burning of the English settlement at Saco. He is reported to have released one young girl taken captive after her family was killed, an act that caused chronicler William Hubbard to describe Squando as "a strange mixture of mercy and cruelty." His abilities in war gained him the characterization of "diabolical miscreant," yet Hubbard also reports that the sachem opposed cruelty and murder against those opponents who were willing to yield to him.

In 1676 Squando was among the signers of a peace treaty with the English at Cochecho.

SQUANTO (Pawtuxet; *c.* 1590– November, 1622),—who served as a slave, a guide, and an interpreter—is best rememberd for his role of savior of the infant Plymouth colony. Much of Squanto's early life is veiled in mystery. He may have been picked up from the coast of Maine in 1605 and carried off to England, from which he returned to Cape Cod in 1615 with Captain John Smith. It is known for certain, however, that Squanto was one of 24 natives kidnapped by Thomas Hunt in 1615. Hunt sold the Indians into slavery at Malaga, Spain, but some of the natives were ransomed and freed by monks. Squanto was taken to England, where he spent two years learning the language and the customs of the English.

In 1619 Squanto returned to the coast of North America, but he discovered that all of the coastal tribes had been decimated by a plague; in fact, he was the only Pawtuxet native to survive. Squanto finally joined the Wampanoag tribe in Rhode Island, and he was one of the large number of Wampanoags (including their chief, Massasoit) whom Samoset introduced to the English settlers at Plymouth in 1620. Squanto served as interpreter between the Pilgrims and Chief Massasoit, and it was Squanto's stories of his experiences in England that helped convince Massasoit of the wisdom of an alliance with the rich and powerful newcomers. The result was a treaty of alliance between the Wampanoags and King James I of England.

Squanto stayed with the settlers during the spring of 1621, teaching them how to plant corn, fertilize the crop, and stay alive in the New World. He then guided the colonists through the wilderness to visit Massasoit, a courtesy call which further cemented the amicable relations between the whites and the Wampanoags. There is evidence, though, to indicate that Squanto so exploited his friendship with the Pilgrims as to make himself an object of scorn and hatred among neighboring Indians.

During the spring of 1622, Squanto lied to the Plymouth authorities, telling them that Massasoit was planning hostilities against them. When the Wampanoag chief heard the story, he demanded that the Pilgrims return Squanto to the tribe. The Pilgrims delayed, and soon Squanto was able to patch up his delicate situation with the Wampanoags. In November of the same year, Squanto led an expedition around Cape Cod, serving as both guide and interpreter. Near Chatham Harbor, the sole-surviving Pawtuxet grew sick with a fever. A few days later Squanto died, his last wish being that he might go to the white man's heaven.

STALKER, JACOB (Inuit; 20th century) a river barge mechanic, was elected to the Alaska state legislature in the mid-1960s.

STANDING BEAR (Ponca; *c.* 1829– 1908), Indian name *Ma-chu-nah-zhay* was a Ponca Indian chief whose heroic efforts, aided by sympathetic white people, helped to bring about the first decision by a U.S. court that "an Indian is a person within the meaning of the law."

Noted for their friendliness to whites, the Poncas lived quietly on land confirmed to them by treaty until, on Jan. 15, 1877, their land was given to the Sioux, and the Poncas were ordered removed to Indian Territory in arid Oklahoma. Standing Bear strongly opposed the order to no avail. Within a year, a third of his people had sickened and died, including his own son, whom he was determined to bury back home.

Setting out from Oklahoma in January 1879, Standing Bear and some 30 followers reached their friends on the Omaha Reservation in March, having walked more than 500 miles. They borrowed land, seeds, and equipment and were about to start planting when soldiers from General George Crook's garrison arrived to take the fugitives back to Oklahoma.

Among the white people who came to the imprisoned Indians' defense were a crusading newspaperman, Thomas H. Tibbles, two brilliant lawyers, and a host of ministers and other public-spirited citizens. The two lawyers drew up a petition for *habeas corpus*—Ma-chu-nah-zhay vs. George Crook. On April 18, 1879, Judge Dundy rendered the famous decision that an Indian was a person within the meaning of the law of the United States and that no authority existed for removing any of the prisoners to Indian Territory.

The committee formed in behalf of the Poncas arranged for Standing Bear and Tibbles to attend a series of meetings in the east to raise money to further Indian rights. With them was the beautiful young Omaha Indian girl Susette LaFlesche, popularly known as Bright Eyes, and her brother Francis, the latter as chaperone for his sister (who married Tibbles in 1881) and interpreter for the eloquent Standing Bull. For months the group aroused the interest and admiration of thousands, among them the most distinguished men and women of the day.

Following his last public appearance, before a Senate investigating committee, Standing Bear rejoined his people in Nebraska where he died 30 years later in poverty.

STARR, ORANGE WALTER, (Cherokee; 20th century), was a member of the Oklahoma state Legislature from 1942 to 1946. He has been a county and city physician and he served in the United States Army Medical Corps during World War I.

STEPHEN I (Mosquito; fl. early 19th century), was the Mosquito Indian who was designated regent of the British-controlled Mosquito Coast of Nicaragua in 1800. The only one of his line not to be called king, he succeeded the most capable Mosquito king, George II. Stephen was succeeded in 1816 by George II's son, George III.

STEVENS, ERNEST (Oneida; 20th century), served as an official of the Bureau of Indian Affairs. He also worked with other Indian programs in California.

STEVENS, JOHN W. (Passamaquoddy; August 11, 1933–   ), became chief of the Passamaquoddy Indians of Indian Township, Maine, in 1955. Born in Washington County, Maine, Stevens served with the United States Marines during the Korean War. As tribal chief he has been active in the struggle of Indians against discrimination and poverty.

STEWART, ALBERT (Chickasaw; July 19, 1909–), a member of the Chickasaw tribe, has achieved fame as a concert singer. Born in Wynnewood, Oklahoma, Stewart studied voice in Chicago. With his bass baritone voice he has been featured at various concerts and festivals. He has also appeared on television and in a film, *Rhythm*, produced for school distribution.

STIGLER, WILLIAM G. (Choctaw; July 7, 1891—August 21, 1852) served eight years in the United States House of Representatives as a congressman from Oklahoma. A member of the Choctaw nation, he was born in the town of Stigler, named for his forbears, in Indian Territory (present day Oklahoma). During World War I he was with the United States Army in Europe, achieving the rank of 2nd lieutenant. After his return to Oklahoma, he was admitted to the bar in 1920 and became active in politics, first as city attorney in Stigler and later as a Democratic senator to the Oklahoma state legislature. In 1931 he became president pro tem of the Senate. From 1937 to 1944 he was national attorney of the Choctaw Nation. Returning to political office in 1944 Stigler was elected to fill a vacancy to the United States House of Representatives. He held that office until his death, August 21, 1952, in Stigler.

STOMIKSOSAK (Blood) was chief in the 1830s.

STRONGHEART, NIPO (Yakima; 1891—December 30, 1966), was a Yakima chief who appeared in a number of motion pictures and served as a flim advisor. His acting career included roles in *Across the Wide Missouri* (1951) and *Lone Star* (1951). In addition to film work he was active in the cause of Indian rights. He died at the age of 75.

SUMAC, YMA (Quechua; 20th century), a descendent of the Incas, has achieved notable success as a singer. Her exceptional voice has ranged through four octaves and has reproduced sounds such as birds or drums. She was born Emperatriz Chavarri on September 13, 1928, in Ichoan in the mountains of Peru. Her mother was a Quechua Indian and her father was of mixed Spanish and Indian ancestry. Singing in tribal festivals as a young girl, she came to the attention of the Peruvian Ministry of Education and was sent to Lima to go to school. She sang in concerts and her talent became increasingly recognized when she joined the Compañia Peruana de Arte, a group of Indian singers, dancers, and musicians. In 1942, she married Moises Vivanco De Allende, the leader of the company. (They were divorced in 1957.) The group toured throughout Latin America. In 1946, she and her husband came to the United States. In the ensuing years Yma Sumac performed in concert halls and night clubs in Europe and the Western Hemisphere with her repertoire of ancient Inca melodies. Her appearances in Carnegie Hall and the Hollywood Bowl brought her special acclaim in the United States. In 1950 her record released by Capital, *Voice of the Xtabay*, sold over 500,000 copies. Her career turned to the stage in 1951 with a role in the Broadway musical, *Flahooley*, and to film in 1954 when she played in Paramount's *Secret of the Incas*. The next year she became a United States citizen. With her remarkable and versatile voice she has also performed in opera and appeared on television.

SUNDOWN, ARNOLD (Iroquois; 20th century), an Iroquois silversmith was born on August 4, 1914. He has worked for the Rochester Museum of Arts and Sciences in Rochester, New York.

SWIMMER (Cherokee) or *Ayunini* was James Mooney's principal informant.

Sacajawea

Sainte Marie, Buffy

SAMOSET, THE INDIAN VISITOR.

Samoset

Santantas

Satanta

Scarfaced Charley

Seattle

Sequoyah

Selocta

Short Bull

Shabbona

Shingabawassin

Silverheels, Jay

Sitting Bull

Smith, Nimrod Jarret

Souligny

Spotted Tail

Standing Bear

Stevens, John W.

Stomiksosak

Swimmer

T

TABARI (Carib; ?– June, 1683), was a Carib Indian chief of the Lesser Antilles who in June 1683 was killed along with a large number of other Indians when the British governor of the Leeward Islands, Sir William Stapleton, conducted raids on St. Vincent and Dominica islands, the most populous Carib strongholds.

TABOGA (Chocó; fl. early 16th century), was a Chocó Indian chief of an island in the Gulf of Panama, off Panama's Pacific coast. After Balboa discovered the Pacific in 1513, the Spanish overran Taboga and the smaller neighboring island of Otoque. Both islands take their names from their Indian chiefs.

TAHCHEE (Cherokee; *c.* 1790—1843), born in Alabama, was a western Cherokee chief. His father was Skyugo, a famous Cherokee leader who moved west to Arkansas when Tahchee was a small boy. The family left the ancestral Cherokee land to avoid harassment by white settlers. As a young man Tahchee fought bravely in a war with the Osage. After the war he lived with members of the Osage tribe and learned to speak their language. He was one of the first to join Chief Bowl in Texas after that chief's migration west of the Mississippi in 1794. The migration was the first major one among Cherokees to land west of the Mississippi. Known to his people as Tatsi, meaning Dutch, he stayed with Chief Bowl for several years. He later returned to Cherokee land to harass Osage Indians living in neighboring areas. His raids were so bold and successful that a $500 reward was offered for his capture by the U.S. At one point he attacked a party of Osage within hearing distance of Fort Gibson.

Eventually he was promised amnesty and settled with his followers southwest of Fort Gibson. He became a scout and guide for the soldiers there. In 1834 his portrait was painted by George Catlin. He died in about 1843.

TAIMAH (Fox; fl. early 19th century), also spelled Taima, Tama, and Taiomah, was chief and medicine man of the Thunder branch who ruled a village near present Burlington, Iowa. A friend to the white settlers, he was responsible for once saving the Indian agent residing at Prairie du Chien, Wisconsin. With Keokuk and other Sauk and Fox chiefs he signed the Washington August 4, 1824 treaty rescinding all claims to lands west of the Mississippi River in Missouri. Taimah died in his village shortly after 1824. The county and town of Tama, Iowa are named for him.

TAKATOKA (Cherokee; ?– ?), an important chief of the Western Cherokee, his name translated to mean *one human body formed by two distinct individuals standing so close together as to be totally unified.*

TALKHORSE (Montauk) or *Stephen Pharoah* was the last king of the Montauks.

TALL BULL (Cheyenne; ?–July 11, 1869), Indian name Hotoa-qa-ihoois a chief of the northern Cheyenne Dog Soldiers, but not of his tribe, played a leading roll in the hostilities of 1868–69.

Actually, the name Tall Bull was hereditary among the Cheyenne at different times, but the subject of this biography was among the most distinguished. He was with Roman Nose in the Beecher Island fight of September 1868. Roman Nose went into battle following the accidental eating of food that had been touched with a metal utensil, thus destroying the magic of his war bonnet. Tall Bull urged him to go through the purification rites necessary to restore his protection. Had Roman Nose taken his friend's advice, he might have lived to fight another day. He was killed early in the fight.

Tall Bull's band continued its savage raids along the Kansas border. In the summer of 1869 General Eugene A. Carr, accompanied by a battalion of Pawnee scouts, trailed the band to Summit Springs. The Indian camp, consisting of 85 lodges, was caught by surprise. In the confusion, Tall Bull managed to catch horses for his wife and six-year-old daughter and ride for a nearby ravine, where he concealed his family, stabbed his horse, and prepared to die, for the Indians were hopelessly outnumbered.

Watching the ravine, Major Frank North saw a rifle appear over the edge of the bank, followed by a head. His aim was deadly, for the body found below that spot proved to be that of Tall Bull. Very soon, another Indian head appeared at the same spot. It belonged to Tall Bull's wife, who, pulling her little girl along, made signs of peace and begged for mercy, which was granted. Of the two white women captives in the Indian camp, one apparently was shot to death by Tall Bull before he departed.

TALLCHIEF, MARIA (Osage; 1925–   ), as one of the world's greatest ballerinas, has achieved professional heights that few have equalled.

She was born in the town of Fairfax, on the Osage Reservation in Oklahoma. She was named Elizabeth Marie Tall Chief and called Betty Marie. There were two other children — Gerald, an older brother, and Marjorie, a younger sister, who was also to become a famous ballerina.

The Tall Chief family was socially prominent. Her father, Alexander, was a chief of the tribe, and her mother Ruth (Porter), a non-Indian, was a leader in community activities. The home was one of culture and the children were raised in an atmosphere typical of any well-to-do family in a small community.

Although her father had been raised in Osage

tradition, Betty Marie knew little of Osage customs, and nothing of the Osage language. Sometimes her grandmother would take her to Indian dances where she absorbed the color and the sounds of the chants and drums. Beyond this, Osage ways were as foreign to her as they would be to any other stranger.

When she was a tiny child, Betty Marie began to pick out tunes on the piano and it was discovered that she had the rare gift of perfect pitch. Piano lessons were started at once and it was planned that she would be a concert pianist. A year later, she began to take dancing lessons. In this, too, she showed a marked ability.

When she was eight, the family moved to Beverly Hills, California, where she was enrolled in the ballet school of Ernest Belcher, a top ballet teacher and in the Los Angeles Conservatory of Music. From then on, her life was one of continuous practice in both arts. There was little time for any childhood or "growing up" pleasures.

Until she was twelve, she was torn between a musical career, as her mother wished, and a dancing one. Then, during a musical-dance recital, her feelings crystallized and she knew that only dancing held any meaning for her.

At fourteen, she was a pupil of Madame Nijinska, the sister of the great Russian dancer, Nijinsky. A strict disciplinarian, Madame Nijinska set in Betty Marie the elements of greatness and she held her constantly to a high standard. She arranged for her to take additional studies with David Lichine, a choreographer who had danced with Pavlova.

When she was still in high school, Maria was given her first opportunity of significance. She was chosen for a solo part in Nijinska's ballet, *Chopin Concerto*. The ballet was performed in the Hollywood Bowl and the critics agreed that the young artist had a distinct future.

After graduation, she was a background dancer in a Judy Garland movie. Then, she went to New York City hoping to become a member of the Ballet Russe.

A number of discouraging months went by before she was finally accepted by the Ballet Russe Company for a Canadian tour. On this tour, Betty Marie made an excellent impression. Though only a corps dancer, she stood out from the rest and soon was given bit parts.

In Montreal, she danced her first important role in *The Snow Maiden*, and again there were predictions of a great future.

Back in New York she was given a year's contract with Ballet Russe and the prominence of advancement as she perfected her skill. She embarked on a period of intense self-discipline, rigorous and constant training and practice, and a life completely dedicated to her art. She met with bitter disappointments, jealousy, and unhappiness along the way, but none of this could swerve her from the course she had set for herself.

She continued to stand out as a corps dancer, and in emergencies, she was pushed into solo parts. As she won attention, she was told that better parts would surely come and she was urged to change her name to a Russian-sounding one, for the Ballet Russe was a Russian company.

This she refused to do, but finally agreed to a compromise, selecting the name of Maria Tallchief. It was purely and proudly Indian.

Six months after her arrival in New York City, Maria was given a small part in *Rodeo*; a new ballet which was an instant success. But long, barren months followed that with Maria still in the corps and no more parts in sight.

Then she was given the role in the *Chopin Concerto* that she had first danced when she was fifteen. This came about because the star in the role had injured her foot. In this part, Maria was at once recognized as a great dancer with the promise of becoming a prima ballerina. In the ballet world, there is no higher, nor more hard-won title.

Maria debuted the *Concerto* role in New York City and received an ovation. Whenever this ballet was announced people flocked to see her. A new star had catapaulted onto the scene and for Maria life would never be the same again.

Later, she came to the attention of George Balanchine who had joined the Ballet Russe as director of the company. He selected her for a part in *Ballet Imperial*, one of his creations, but the work was not suited to her and she made only a lukewarm impression. Then she was cast in *Les Sylphidies*, and achieved a sensational performance. The critics raved and wondered if she could ever again repeat a performance so magical. She did not disappoint them.

More and more important roles came her way and so marvelously did Balanchine bring her out, that the two were the talk of the ballet world. Then she was cast in the extremely difficult role of the fairy in *Le Baiser de la Feé*. This role had been performed by only the most expert of ballerinas. Balanchine choreographed the role especially for her and her dancing of it was so stupendous that it would never again be equalled by any one. The theatre rocked with cheers.

After this, she was starred in Balanchine's *Night Shadow* and again she was hailed with delight.

In 1946, Maria Tallchief and Balanchine were married. She was now a star of first rank — the only American ballerina in history.

With their marriage, the Balanchine's left the Ballet Russe company to join a new one called Ballet Society. They went to Paris where Maria again appeared in the fairy role and enchanted the sophisticated Parisian audiences, prepared to look down their noses at an American dancer.

Returning to New York, she was starred in *Orpheus*, and was breathtaking. For this role, she received the American Dance Magazine award and opened a new era in dramatic ballet.

For a brief period, Maria was a guest ballerina with Ballet Theatre. Then it was announced that Balanchine would present her in *The Firebird*. Audiences that had wondered if she could re-create the splendor of her appearances for Ballet Theatre were frankly skeptical that the Russian folk tale would be suitable for her. Maria, herself, was in awe of the role.

But Balanchine knew that she would go far above and beyond anything that she had ever done before. The ballet made history and it made Maria Tallchief one of the great artists of all time. Now she danced only the choicest roles.

But fame did not bring happiness and the great tragedy of her life was the ending of her marriage to Balanchine, although a professional relationship continued. As she recovered from this shattering blow, she was partnered with André Eglevsky and the two were incomparable, their appearances a triumphant procession in the major European cities.

Then Maria married Elmourza Natirboff, a charter airline pilot. But this was doomed from the start by the demands of her career. She was hailed and wanted the world over, and tributes poured in from every part of the globe.

The state of Oklahoma declared "Maria Tallchief Day". The Osage tribe, in special ceremonies, gave her the title of Princess and the name of *Wa-Xthe-Thoma*, or Woman of Two Standards. She was named Woman of the Year by the Woman's National Press Club. She was given the Indian Achievement Award. The list of honors is a lengthy one.

The trauma of the breakup of her marriage eventually brought her to new peaks, for she emerged from the experience as a stronger, finer person and a dancer of such emotional depth and sensitivity that she could perform any role.

Balanchine now presented her as the Sugar Plum Fairy in *The Nutcracker*. Again she reached new heights of glory and the clamor to see her was unabating. She joined the New York City Ballet for a European tour, she appeared in South America, Japan and the Middle East, and in more than 100 American cities. She was the undisputed and unchallenged queen of the ballet.

In 1956, still wearing her crown, she married Henry Paschen, a Chicago business man. After the birth of her daughter Elisa Maria, she returned to New York City Ballet to fulfill her commitments. She now danced with Erik Bruhn and this partnership was declared the greatest in ballet history. After a tour of Europe and Russia, she was assigned to appear in *Miss Julie* and once more surpassed herself.

With this as her final triumph, she decided to retire and devote herself to being wife and mother. Retirement did not mean inactivity, however. She is the mistress of two beautiful homes, a leader in social and civic affairs, and a lecturer and teacher before university and college groups. She makes frequent appearances on educational TV programs, and is interested in establishing a Chicago ballet company.

Since her retirement there has been no cessation of honors. A number of colleges and universities have awarded her honorary degrees. She received the coveted Cappezio Dance Award and the award of the National Institute of Arts and Letters and was chosen one of the "Legendary Women of America." She will remain an ideal and example for generations of dancers far into the future.

TALLCHIEF, MARJORIE (Osage; 1927–   ), a ballerina of international fame, was born in Denver, Colorado. Her father was an Osage Indian and her mother was of Scotch-Irish extraction. Both she and her sister Maria were serious students of ballet together as children and Marjorie joined the American Ballet Theater when she was nineteen. In 1947, she married George Skibine with whom she has danced in many ballets. She has been prima ballerina in a number of ballet companies including the American Ballet Theater, Ballet de Monte Carlo, and L'Opéra de Paris. In the course of her work she has created several leading parts such as Medusa in *Undertow* and the title role in *Ariadne*. She has received acclaim for her performances in both classical and contemporary ballets.

TAMAHA (Sioux; 1775–1860), or 'rising moose' was a noted chief of the Medwakanton Sioux, who lived in the region of Blue Earth and Mille Lacs in Minnesota. He was born on the site of Winona, Minn., and in the early part and middle of the last century was one of the chief men of his tribe. He seems to have maintained throughout his long life an excellent reputation for honesty. In childhood, while at play, he sustained the loss of an eye, on which account the French nicknamed him "Le Borgne," or "One Eye," and the English "the One-Eyed Sioux." In 1806–07 he met and formed a great admiration for Lieut. Z. M. Pike, and so constantly did he sing the praises of his white friend that the Indians, with a sense of humor worthy a modern punster, changed the pronunciation of the last syllable of his name from *haw* to *hay*, which made the name signify "pike," the fish. Because of his attachment for Pike, he is said to have been the only Sioux Indian, with one exception, whose sympathies were with the Americans, and who did active service for them during the War of 1812. In this crisis, when Joseph Renville and the old Little Crow led their Sioux followers against the United States forces, Tahama refused to join them. At this period he made his way to St. Louis, and at the solicitation of General Clarke, then Indian Commissioner, he entered the service of the United States as a scout and messenger. He returned in 1814 with Manuel Lisa, when the latter was on his way to confer with the Missouri River Indians, and, parting with him at the mouth of the James River, carried dispatches to the Americans at Prairie du Chien, Wis. Through privations and discouragements he remained loyal to the United States and faithfully performed the duties assigned him. While on one of his trips to Prairie du Chien, Tamaha was imprisoned by Col. Robert Dickson, an Indian trader, and at that time an officer in the service of the British, who, under threat of death, attempted to compel him to divulge information relative to the Americans; but Tamaha would not yield. After a term of imprisonment he was released and again visited St. Louis in 1816. On this visit he was present at the council held by General Clarke with the forty-six chiefs from the upper Missouri, who had returned with Manuel Lisa. On this occasion General Clarke presented him with a medal of honor and a captain's uniform, and commissioned him chief of the Sioux nation. He is said to have been a man of fine physique and much natural dignity, and an orator of unusual ability. One of his peculiarities was to always wear a stovepipe hat. Until his death, at Wabasha, Minn., at the age of 85, he was much respected, not only by the whites but by his own people. His name is also written Tahama, Tahamie, Tammahaw. By the French he was called Original Levé, the translation of his native designation.

TAMAQUE (Delaware; *c.* 1725–*c.* 1770), also The Beaver and King Beaver was alternately friendly and hostile to 18th century English settlers along the frontier. Brother of Shingass, a merciless and treacherous enemy of colonial pioneers in western Pennsylvania, Tamaque was—like his brother—an important Delaware chieftain. Moving to Ohio following the British occupation of Fort Duquesne, he settled near the junction of the Tuscarawas and Big Sandy at a village called *The Beaver's Town*. There he carried on friendly relations with the English until 1755, but following British General Braddock's defeat at the hands of a combined French and Indian force, Tamaque switched his alliance from the English to the French. By 1758 the chief was expressing his desire to resume good relations with the English, and he attended a council at Fort Pitt in 1759 and another in 1760 to further this desire. In 1762 Tamaque promised the colonial governor of Pennsylvania that the Delaware under his command would return all captured whites held as prisoners, but he then joined enthusiastically in Pontiac's conspiracy, leading several Indian raids against frontier settlements. When Pontiac's plans to drive the English out of the Great Lakes region met defeat, however, the fickle Tamaque again agreed to keep the peace. His years of war-making done, the Delaware chief permitted himself to be converted to Christianity by Moravian missionaries and spent his final years as a zealous advocate of his new faith.

TAMMANY (Delaware; fl. 17th century), appears to have been two Tammanys—an imaginary figure and a real one—but the mythology associated with the former became embellished and associated with the latter.

The imaginary Tammany, a leader among the legendary mound builders, is supposed to have lived west of the Alleghenies in pre-Columbian times. He was a sagacious, charitable, superhuman protagonist against a satanic being called the *Evil Spirit* who wanted to destroy the Indians. The *Evil Spirit* sent poisonous serpents, herds of mammoths and other monsters to consume the Indians' corn, and noxious plants to spread disease and plague. Tammany repulsed all these forces, and when the *Evil Spirit* raised the waters of Lake Huron and Michigan to flood the land and drown the Indians, Tammany diverted the waters to form the Miami, Wabash, Allegheny, and other rivers. The rapids of Detroit and the falls of the Niagara are the result of his handiwork. He was widely hailed as the saviour of the Indians, and even the Great Inca of Peru is supposed to have heard of his fame, and sent for him to meet him in Mexico to consult about the principles of a government for the Peruvians.

All of these myths, and much more, which have no historical foundation, were fabricated to exalt Tammany and rationalize his elevation to the status of an Indian patron saint. Dr. Samuel Latham Mitchell, a college professor, in a speech delivered in New York City May 12, 1795, generated many of these Tammany fables which others enlarged.

The real Tammany (whose name also appears in contemporary documents as Tamanend, Taminy, Taminent, Tamanee, and Tamina) was one of a number of band chiefs among the historic Delaware Indians (also known as the *Lenni Lenape*) in the late seventeenth century. Tammany's name has been said to mean "affable," but this is speculative because the original pronunciation is uncertain, and the Delawares had no system of writing to preserve the correct orthography.

Despite the fact that recorded data about him is very meager, Tammany's name has become associated with extraordinary deeds and unusual sagacity. He is often referred to as the head chief of the Delaware Nation, which is incorrect because the Delawares did not have one principle leader until many years later.

The date and place of Tammany's birth are unknown. He appears first on the pages of history in May of 1683 when he and two other Delaware sachems, Hetkoquean and Menanget, conferred with William Penn at the Indian town of Perkasie, about thirty miles north of Philadelphia in present Hilltown Township, Bucks County, Pennsylvania.

On June 23, 1683, Tammany and another chief named Metamequan sold their respective lands to William Penn. In exchange for his hunting territory lying between Neshaminy Creek in Bucks County, and Pennypack Creek in Philadelphia County, Tammany received a quantity of blankets, metal axes, stockings, hats, combs, looking glasses, shirts, iron kettles, guns, and other European merchandise which the chief considered a valuable payment for the land. The deed with Tammany's mark on it, and a receipt for the goods drawn up by William Penn in his own hand have been preserved in the state records at Harrisburg.

On June 15, 1692, Tammany and three other Delaware band or village chiefs (all four are referred to by the white scribe as "Indian kings") sold additional land in Bucks County to representatives of the Penn government for appropriate European goods.

On July 5, 1697, Tammany again received additional payment in English merchandise for the land he had previously sold. This deed of sale refers to his brother Weheeland, alias Andrew, and his two sons, Yaqueekhon, who had adopted the English name Nicholas, and Quenameckquid, known as Charles. Nothing is known about these three Indians, nor was the name of Tammany's wife, or daughters, if any, recorded.

After Tammany and his family had consumed, or worn out the European goods, he evidently regretted disposing of his lands. When English families began to settle in Bucks County he tried to stop them and threatened to burn their houses. The Commissioners of Property presented him with six guns, ten blankets, ten kettles, and some bread and beer. This seemed to pacify him, and he allowed the settlers to build their homes unmolested.

Only one of Tammany's utterances has been recorded. On July 6, 1694, he and several other Delaware chiefs had an audience with Governor William Markham in Philadelphia for the purpose of renewing the bonds of friendship. Two of the chiefs made speeches, which were followed by some remarks by Tammany. His words, couched in the metaphorical language of his tribe, are given below as they were spelled and recorded by the translator:

"Wee and the Christians of this river [the Delaware] Have allwayes had a free rode to one another, & tho' sometimes a tree has fallen across the rode yet wee have still removed it again & keept the path clean, and wee design to Continou the old friendshipp that has been between us and you."

The date and place of Tammany's death are not known, but he was not living when William Penn made his second visit to Pennsylvania in 1699. He died either late in 1697, or in 1698, probably in advanced years. Local tradition recorded by the late Henry C. Mercer has it that he was buried near a spring on the right bank of Neshaminy Creek, New Britain Township, Bucks County, but the grave has never been found. A far-fetched story says that having accomplished all he could in the way of imparting wisdom to his tribe he became a martyr by burning himself to death. The inventor of this tale probably confused Tammany with another Delaware chief Teedyuskung who was burned to death in his cabin April 19, 1763.

Almost a hundred years after Tammany's death, May 1, later changed to May 12, began to be celebrated in his honor, first in Philadelphia. During the Revolution Pennsylvania troops chose him as their patron saint, and soon St. Tammany's Day was observed in the colonies by soldiers and civilians alike. How this cannonization came about still remains to be satisfactorily explained. In 1789, a resident of New York city, William Mooney, organized a patriotic and fraternal order called *The Society of Tammany or Columbian Order* in which Tammany and Columbus were co-saints. Tammany's name was later transferred to a powerful New York political machine called Tammany Hall.

TANTAQUIDGEON, GLADYS (Mohegan; June 5, 1899 –   ), a Mohegan and one of the first Indians to become an anthropologist, was born in New London, Connecticut. A tenth generation descendant of Uncas of James Fenimore Cooper's *Last of the Mohicans*, she has written articles on ethnological and antropological subjects, dealing particularly with the Mohegans. With her brother Harold she is curator of the Tantaquidgeon Indian Museum in Uncasville, Connecticut.

TANTAQUIDGEON, HAROLD (Mohegan; June 18, 1904–   ), a Mohegan, is curator with his sister Gladys of the Tantaquidgeon Indian Museum in Uncasville, Connecticut.Born in Montville, Connecticut, he served as a tail gunner in World War II and fought again in the Korean conflict. His work at the museum has included lecturing on the history of the Mohegans and other tribes in the area.

TARHE (Wyandot; 1742– November, 1818), also known as the Crane, born in Detroit, was a Wyandot chief and head priest of the Porcupine branch, and was a strong opponent of Tecumseh. In 1774 he fought under the Shawnee chief Cornstalk at the battle of Point Pleasant in present West Virginia. He served under Blue Jacket at the Battle of Fallen Timbers, Ohio, August 20, 1794, and, although seriously wounded, was the only chief to escape. In 1795, resisting tribal opposition, he was a leader in the negotiations that resulted in the August 3, Treaty of Greenville, Ohio signed by 12 Indian tribes, that delineated the boundaries between the tribes and the territory open to U.S. settlers. As a result of this treaty Tarhe became a U.S. pensioner.

Tarhe was a leader in the opposition to Tecumseh's plans. Although he too was aware of the continued encroachments by whites upon Indian lands, he refused to join Tecumseh. Acting for the U.S. government, Tarhe called a meeting of Northwest

Indian chiefs loyal to the U.S. at Brownstown on the Detroit River to plead for their continued neutrality. At the same time Tecumseh, in response to Tarhe's actions called a meeting of anti-U.S. chiefs at Amherstburg, Ontario, Canada across the Detroit River from Brownstown. Although Tecumseh soon invaded the Brownstown encampment and pressed many of the chiefs into joining him, Tarhe fled upon learning of the imminent attack and avoided facing Tecumseh. During the War of 1812 Tarhe led his warriors in the service of Gen. William H. Harrison in his campaign into Canada, and helped defeat Tecumseh at the October 5, 1813 Battle of the Thames River.

After the War, Tarhe returned to central Ohio where he became well known to the white settlers. His friendship was held highly by everyone, and especially by Harrison. Tarhe died at Cranetown near Upper Sandusky, Ohio.

TASCALUSA (Alibamu; fl. 16th century), on October 18, 1540, led his tribe in combat against the Spanish invaders under the command of Hernando De Soto, a conflict described by historian George Bancroft as probably the greatest single Indian battle ever fought within the boundaries of what would later become the United States. The chief, a tall, strong, handsome man, refused the Spaniards' demand that the Alibamu supply the invading Europeans with provisions and laborers, and he scoffed with contempt when they tried to intimidate him with a show of horsemanship. When personally threatened by De Soto, however, Tascalusa seemed to submit, telling the Spanish commander that he would send messengers to the Indian town of Mabila with orders to prepare the men and supplies demanded. What Tascalusa actually instructed the messengers to relay, though, was a call to all Alibamu warriors to assemble at Mabila and prepare for war.

When the first Spaniards arrived at the Indian

village, they unloaded their baggage in the public square and then witnessed an apparently friendly dance of welcome. But during the dance some of the soldiers spotted warriors stockpiling bows and arrows, and they discovered armed natives hiding near the roof of a house. Immediately, De Soto—who had not yet entered Mabila—prepared his defenses and called for Tascalusa to come to him. When the chief refused and the Spaniards attempted to capture him, the battle of Mabila was on.

The Indians quickly drove the Spanish advance guard out of their town, set free the natives who had previously been taken and enslaved by the invaders, and armed these fellow natives with bows and arrows to fight the white men. Their success within Mabila was reversed, however, when the Alibamu pursued their enemies into the open countryside. There the Spanish cavalry—equipped with iron armor, swords, and long lances—gained the upper hand over the naked natives fighting on foot with bows and arrows.

The battle lasted an entire day. Finally, the Spaniards succeeded in setting Mabila on fire and in driving the last desperate Alibamu defenders back into the blazing village. When defeat became inevitable, many Indians—women and children as well as warriors—committed suicide rather than submit to the Spanish conquerors. At least 2500 Alibamu died in the battle of Mabila, including Tascalusa's son whose body was discovered with a lance thrust through it. Tascalusa's body was never found, and the chief's fate remains a mystery.

TATARRAX (Pawnee; fl. 16th century), visited Coronado in 1541 during the Spanish conqueror's expedition to Quivira. Summoned by Coronado, who was camped along the Kansas River, Tatarrax brought along approximately 200 warriors armed with bows and arrows. A monument to his memory was erected at Manhattan, Kansas in 1905.

TATEMY (Delaware; *c.* 1700–1761), a Delaware chief, served as an interpreter on several occasions in colonial Pennsylvania. Following his early interpreting assignments for the Province of Pennsylvania, Tatemy received a land grant of 300 acres in Northampton County. His home there became a popular meeting place, especially for those visitors traveling to and from the Moravian settlements of Nazareth and Bethlehem. He continued to serve as an interpreter and spokesman for his tribe at various treaty negotiations.

TAVIBO (Paiute; fl. 19th century), became a cult figure during the middle of the 19th century, following his claims to receiving divine revelations portraying the destruction of the whites and the resurrection of the Indians. Already enjoying fame as a medicine man, Tavibo became even more prominent when he went up into the mountains and returned with the prophecy that a giant earthquake would destroy all the white people, leaving the land to the dispossessed Indians. His message heartened those natives—Shoshoni, Bannock, and Paiute—whose lands in the mountain valleys had recently been taken over by white settlers. Some Indians were skeptical, however, failing to comprehend how an earthquake of such magnitude as to swallow up all the whites would not consume the natives as well. Tavibo replied with a second revelation in which no such discrimination took place during the earthquake, but which instead predicted a happy resurrection of the Indians after the disaster subsided. Although the medicine man acquired a large following—believers flocking to him from Nevada, Idaho, and Oregon—he fell from favor when the predicted earthquake failed to occur. As his popularity waned, Tavibo offered a third prophecy: the promised earthquake would swallow up white and Indian alike as before, but only those natives who had believed in Tavibo would be resurrected.

TAZA (Apache; ?– November 15, 1876), also Tahza, Tahzay and Tahza was the eldest son of Chief Cochise, who in 1876 masterminded the disappearance of his own clan of 38 Chiricahua. Enroute to San Carlos Reservation, they fled south to Sonora, Mexico, where they referred to themselves as "The Nameless Ones." Chief Taza headed a delegation of 20 Apache to visit President Ulysses S. Grant in Washington, where he took pneumonia and died. Angered, Taza's brother Naiche, with other chieftains, bolted the San Carlos Reservation and began the legendary Geronimo wars that lasted for ten years.

TE ATA (Chickasaw; 20th century), has achieved prominence as an interpreter of Indian folklore. A Chickasaw, she was born in Tishomingo, Oklahoma. She took an interest in acting while in school and went to New York City for further training. In 1933 she married Clyde Fisher, director of the Hayden Planetarium and the American Museum of Natural History. Among other roles she appeared on the New York stage as Andromache in *The Trojan Women*. Later she created a program of dramatic presentations of Indian folklore and chants, which she has performed in the United States and Europe.

TEBBEL, JOHN (Ojibwa; November 16, 1912–), a professor of journalism at New York University, has written many books on journalism and United States history. A descendant of an Ojibwa chief, he was born in Boyne City, Michigan. Before he entered academia his journalism career included positions at *Newsweek*, *The Detroit Free Press*, and *The New York Times*. From 1943 to 1945 he was an assistant professor of journalism at the School of Journalism at Columbia University and in 1954 he became chairman of the Department of Journalism at New York University. He gave up the chairmanship in 1965 but remains professor of journalism there. His published work has ranged from such topics as *George Horace Lorimer and the Saturday Evening Post* (1948) to *A History of Book Publishing in the United States* (1972). He has also written on Indian history and has contributed articles to a number of periodicals.

TECHOLATLLATZIN (Chichimec; fl. 12th century), was the fifth Chichimec ruler at Texcoco in the 12th century who learned the Toltec language and welcomed learned and civilized men to his city, gradually incorporating them into his tribe. Techolatllatzin was an important transition figure between the barbarian Chichimecs who first invaded the Valley of Mexico and their urbane, spohisticated, and literary descendents at Texaco.

TECUMSEH (Shawnee; March 1768– Oct. 5, 1813) distinguished himself as a brave and merciful warrior, but his greatness rests primarily on his attempt to forge an independent Indian nation in the Northwest Territory. He was born at Old Piqua, Ohio, in 1768. The murder of his father at the hands of white frontiersmen filled young Tecumseh with hatred toward the Americans, and his animosity increased during savage border warfare between the Shawnee and the Kentucky and Ohio settlers. Yet, despite his hostility toward Americans, Tecumseh opposed the traditional practice of torturing prisoners; his compassion and integrity, in fact, stirred the admiration of his fiercest enemies.

During the 1780s, Tecumseh formed his own band of warriors and conducted guerilla-style raids against the white settlements that encroached upon Shawnee territory. He joined the inter-tribal force in November 1791 that destroyed the 2,000-man army of Gen. Arthur St. Clair, sent to suppress the sort of native resistance in which Tecumseh had already distinguished himself. The massacre of St. Clair's army put a temporary halt to the expansion of American settlement in the Northwest Territory.

Tecumseh increased his reputation for bravery against Gen. Anthony Wayne's forces at the Battle of Fallen Timbers (August 20, 1794), but the Indians were badly mauled and forced to retreat further westward. The following year, a number of chiefs signed the Greenville Treaty, ceding to the United States enormous tracts of Indian land in Ohio, Indiana, Illinois, and Michigan. Tecumseh refused to attend the peace council, and he similarly refused to be bound by what the chiefs had given away.

As a leader of Indian resistance to land cessions, Teceumseh now emerged as the dominant native chief in the northwest. Although he was forced to move westward himself, he began to acquire a following of other warriors who would not accept the provisions of the Greenville Treaty. Around the turn of the century, Tecumseh developed a coherent philosophical and political program for the Indians' defense of their land. He stated that all tribal land was owned in common and that no chief could sell any parcel of it unless all tribes agreed. In essence, therefore the only way that white settlers could acquire native land was through conquest, and Tecumseh now devoted himself to forming a vast Indian confederation that would repel further white advances. The Shawnee chief became, in effect, a great nationalist, trying to erect an independent Indian nation before all the tribes were swept away in the flood of westward settlement.

Tecumseh and his brother, called The Prophet, established the confederation's headquarters (called Prophet's Town) along the Tippecanoe River in Indiana, and then set out to unite as many tribes as possible in a mutual defense pact. In addition, Tecumseh attempted to instill a sense of pride in native traditions and to urge his brethren to abandon the liquor for which they were rapidly trading all their possessions and territory.

Tecumseh and The Prophet traveled from village to village and achieved remarkable success. In 1809

Tecumseh even went to Florida in order to win Seminole allegiance to his confederation, but in 1811 William Henry Harrison smashed the confederation's headquarters at Tippecanoe. While Tecumseh was away once again on a mission of unification, his brother had foolishly provoked Harrison into an attack that leveled Prophet's Town and scattered Tecumseh's followers.

Harrison's victory, while little more than a minor border incident in itself, was fatal to Tecumseh's dream of a permanent Indian nation. Soon, isolated bands of warriors resumed their guerilla warfare to which the American military forces responded. The Shawnee chief's vision of a united defense of tribal territory was never to be realized. Instead, Tecumseh led his followers to the British army during the War of 1812, confident that a British victory would halt the American assaults upon Indian land. After repeatedly distinguishing himself in battle, Tecumseh finally was slain by Harrison's forces at the Battle of the Thames River in Ontario in October 1813. Never again would there be significant Indian resistance in the Northwest Territory, although Tecumseh remained a symbol of greatness to his dispersed descendents.

TEEDYUSCUNG (Delaware; *c.* 1700–1763), was a Delaware Indian leader in colonial Pennsylvania during the period of the land cessions and frontier wars which forced these Indians westward toward the Ohio country. He advocated a policy of resistance to white pressures and attained notoriety as a Delaware spokesman at numerous treaties and councils.

Teedyuscung was born about 1700 in New Jersey, near present-day Trenton, and lived with his kinfolk in the remnant Indian community there until about 1830, when the family moved across the Delaware River and settled along the Lehigh Valley. From this location the Indians were ousted in

1737 by the so-called Walking Purchase. The purchase allegedly covering these lands actually had been made years before but it was not until 1737 that, according to the provisions of a later agreement, two white men well-supplied walked off its extent in a day-and-a-half. The Indians protested, charging that the intent had been to alienate far less land, and that the government of Pennsylvania was perpetrating a fraud. Resentment over the Walking Purchase was in large part responsible for Teedyuscung's and other Delaware Indian's demands at later treaties and eventually for the defection of Teedyuscung's band to the French side during the French and Indian War.

At first, however, Teedyuscung attempted to remain on the lands. But white settlers began to enter the Forks of the Delaware, and the Iroquois—who claimed an authority of sorts over the Delaware—in 1742 ordered the Delaware of the Forks to vacate their lands, and in 1749 the Iroquois purported to sell these and other lands to the Penns. Many of the Indians now left for new homes on the Susquehanna. But Teedyuscung remained, converting to the Moravian faith and going to live in the communal settlement of some 500 Christian Indians at Gnadenhütten, north of the Moravian headquarters at Bethlehem. He remained there until 1754, when along with most of the others, under Iroquois insistence, he removed to Wyoming, on the Susquehanna (where Wilkes-Barre now stands). His political career dates from that removal.

Before 1754 and his death in 1763, Teedyuscung was active as a council speaker for the Delaware Indians of Wyoming. During the hostilities on Pennsylvania's frontier, he was a warrior and leader of the warrior's faction of the Wyoming Delaware. The policy of this faction was to use the military crisis to extort concessions from the province of Pennsylvania, threatening (and occasionally carrying out) reprisal raids if redress were not offered for land grievances and if Pennsylvania did not cease to endorse (or even promote) the Iroquois claims to sovereignty over the Delaware. At a series of council meetings with whites from 1756 to 1760, he articulated the Delaware position in eloquent speeches. These speeches were set down, in English translation, and published in the minutes of Indian treaties printed by Benjamin Franklin. He came thus to be widely known as a persuasive spokesman for the Indian interest.

Teedyuscung was given political support by the Quakers of the province who wanted to embarrass their opponents, the Proprietary party, by publicizing the Delaware charges of misconduct in Indian affairs. This did not endear him to the government of Pennsylvania, or to Sir William Johnson, the Crown's Superintendent of Indian Affairs, and they did much to discredit him. He died at Wyoming, however, in the course of resisting an invasion of that place by Connecticut settlers; it is alleged that he was murdered.

Teedyuscung's diplomacy was unable to prevent the rapid erosion of the Indian position in the east. Whether or not his specific charges were valid, however, he was a widely cited symbol of Indian resistance to white rapacity, because of the publicity given to his cause by the Quakers and the printing of the Indian treaties. He, and other Indian spokesmen like him, were able to inspire sympathizers among the whites who, working within their own political systems, were able to insist on an Indian policy less destructive to the Indians than that desired by many frontiersman and land speculators.

TEEHEE, HOUSTON BENGE (Cherokee; Oktober, 1874– November 19, 1953), held a number of public offices in Oklahoma but achieved national prominence when he served as Registrar of the United States Treasury from 1915 to 1919. A Cherokee Indian, he was born in what is now Sequoyah

County, Oklahoma (formerly Cherokee Nation, Indian Territory). A lawyer by profession, Teehee moved up the ranks in Oklahoma politics as a Democrat, first as alderman and than as mayor of Tahlequah, Oklahoma. In 1911, he was elected to the Oklahoma House of Representatives and, in 1912, to the United States House of Representatives. Before his appointment as Registrar of the Treasury, Teehee served as U. S. S. Probate Attorney for the Cherokee Indians in Oklahoma. As Registrar his signature appeared on billions of dollars worth of government securities. After leaving the government he worked for a group of oil companies. In 1926 he returned to political office as assistant attorney general of Oklahoma and a year later he became a member of the Supreme Court Commission of Oklahoma, a post he held until 1931. Teehee died in Tahlequah.

TEGRAMUND (Carib; fl. 17th century), was a Carib Indian chief of St. Kitts in 1624, when Sir Thomas Warner and the British began colonizing the West Indies. Tegramund cheerfully allowed them to establish the settlement known as Old Road. In 1627, the English and French allied to drive the Indians from the island.

TEHORAGWANEGEN (Iroquois; *c.* 1758– August 16, 1849), also called Thomas Williams, was an Iroquois war chief of the Caughnawaga tribe of Mohawks in Quebec who, during the American Revolution, fought against the Americans but firmly was opposed to the needless killing of women and children carried on by the western Indian warriors under British command. Born around 1758, Tehoragwanegen, through his mother, was the great grandson of Rev. John Williams of Deerfield, Massachusetts and was raised as a Roman Catholic by his aunt Catherine, wife of a Caughnawaga chief.

Gaining the friendship and trust of the British colonial government in Canada during the Revolution, he and his tribe accompanied various expeditions along the northern frontier both participating, and attempting to restrain and prevent unnecessary slaughter and inhumane treatment of prisoners. Joining the campaign around Saratoga, New York (1777), Tehoragwanegen berated Gen. John Burgoyne, who respected him, for permitting his western Ottawa, Chippewa, Menominee, and Winnebago to attack the colonists so viciously. Burgoyne's defeat at Saratoga may have resulted partially from his reprimanding his Indian warriors so strongly that many of them deserted. Similarly, in 1780 Tehoragwanegen reproached Sir John Johnson whose forces were rampaging through the Mohawk Valley. Tehoragwanegen's friendship with the governor of Canada prevented Johnson from breaking off relations with the chief.

After peace was established, in 1783 he visited his relatives in Massachusetts with whom he later (1800) left his two sons to be educated. Tehoragwanegen was instrumental in establishing the negotiations (1789) which resulted in the Treaty of New York (1792) between the state of New York and the neighboring Indian nations of Canada in which the Indians were given compensation for lands lost. He opposed the British and Tecumseh in the War of 1812, but did not take a prominent role in the hostilities. Tehoragwanegen died in Quebec having served as an instrument of restraint throughout the Revolution and as a mediator in establishing and maintaining peaceful relations between whites and Indians.

TENBANTO (Yaqui; ?–July, 1901), more correctly Tetabiate ("Rolling Stone") was the Indian name of the Yaqui leader Juan María Maldonado, who in 1887 succeeded the famous Cajeme as commander of the rebellious Yaqui forces in Mexico's Sonora state. After ten years of severe warfare,

Tetabiate signed in 1897 the Peace of Ortiz with Sonora's governor Luis Torres. 1899 saw the Yaquis again in revolt. On January 18, 1900, Tetabiate suffered a disastrous defeat at the Massacre of Mazocoba. In July 1901, a Mexican army detachment commanded by his former lieutenant Loreto Villa found Tetabiate in hiding and killed him, leaving the Yaqui rebels leaderless.

TENDILE (Aztec; fl. 16th century), also spelled Teuhtile, an Aztec noble who served Moctezuma Xocoyotzin as a governor or tax-gatherer in the province where modern Vera Cruz is located and who was sent to size up the Spanish when they landed.

On April 23, 1519, an Easter Sunday, Tendile and another noble, accompanied by a force of warriors and a scribe to record everything, met Hernán Cortés and began many days of discussion. Tendile shuttled back and forth between Cortés and Moctezuma, who was in Tenochtitlán, serving as a messenger and transporting their gifts to each other. When Moctezuma called off the discussions, Tendile and his Indians disappeared from history.

TENDOY (Lemhi; *c.* 1840– May 9, 1907), earned the gratitude of white settlers in the Lemhi valley for his unwavering devotion to their safety, even during the Nez Percé conflict. As chief of a mixed band (Bannock, Shoshoni, and Tukuarika), Tendoy was often advised to generate hostilities against the whites, on the theory that a troublesome chief commanded more respect from the federal government—and, consequently, received a larger appropriation for his tribe. But Tendoy would have none of it, telling those persons who volunteered such advice: "I have not the blood of a white man in my camp, nor do I intend such." Not only did Tendoy never initiate a war on whites, but he also protected the settlers against roving bands of hostile Indians.

During the warfare between the U.S. Army and the Nez Perce, moreover, Tendoy prevented any of his people from joining the Indian uprising, and due to his control over his followers, no white person in the Lemhi valley was harmed. Upon the chief's death in 1907, the grateful settlers donated money to buy a tract of land for Tendoy's burial place, and they erected a monument to honor their faithful friend.

TENOCH (Aztec; fl. 14th century), was most important in the Aztec collective government of four priest-rulers during their residence at Tizaapan. Around 1325 (traditional date) he led the Aztecs to an island in Lake Texcoco where they founded their capital, Tenochtitlán (now Mexico City). Ténoch probably died about 1372.

TENSKWATAWA (Shawnee; 1775– November, 1837), 19th century Shawnee mystic, widely known as The Prophet, lived in parts of present-day Ohio and Indiana. He was defeated by William Henry Harrison at the Battle of Tippecanoe. Tenskwatawa was a fervent advocate of a return to traditional Indian society as a means to expel advancing white civilization from newly ceded Indian lands.

Born Laulewasika (Lalawéthika, Laulewaasikaw [a rattle] in Ohio during the winter of 1775, he was the brother, possibly the twin brother of Tecumseh, a major Pan-Indian leader of the time. Tenskwatawa and Tecumseh worked towards building an integrated, unified Indian people whose group strength would renew Indian integrity and culture thus strengthening their hold over tribal lands. Tenskwatawa, blind in one eye, possessed a charismatic personality that gave rise to fervent followers trusting in his supernatural ability.

During his youth, the Indians of the Ohio and Mississippi valleys witnessed the relentless press westward of white settlers across the Alleghenies. The disunited Indians battled, retreated, and ceded their lands. The Shawnee lost lands north of the Ohio River at the Treaty of Greenville in 1795 and between 1802 and 1809 Governor Harrison of the Indiana Territory obtained additional land-ceding treaties. These treaties caused rising anger and frustration among young Indians.

Little is known of Tenskwatawa's early years when he reportedly suffered from alcoholism. In 1805 at the age of 30 he underwent a transformation after a long trance. He announced that he had entered the spirit world where the 'Master of Life' had revealed to him the way for Indians to preserve their lands.

He began his religious career, changing his name from Laulewasika to Tenskwatawa ('the open door'), meaning the channel of revelation from the 'Master of Life'. Through his prophesies he declared that all facets of white civilization should be rejected: dress, alcohol, and intermarriage. He discouraged Indian witchcraft and advocated deposing those chiefs who had granted land concessions. Tenskwatawa's words were a magnet to disillusioned young Indians and the movement became a reactionary message to return to the customs and traditions of old.

Tenskwatawa was soon known as The Prophet. He united with the political movement of Tecumseh, a powerful and eloquent Indian spokesman of the then Northwest Territory. In November of 1805 the two brothers assembled their followers at Wapakoneta (now Greenville, Ohio). While his brother traveled throughout the Mississippi Valley and the southeast urging unity, Tenskwatawa continued to make prophetic announcements. He reportedly gained wide acceptance by predicting the eclipse of the sun of the summer of 1806.

Governor Harrison became alarmed at the brothers' growing popularity. He felt they were being encouraged by the British for an eventual takeover of their ceded lands. Governmental pressure was applied on the settlement. Tecumseh and

Tenskwatawa, not wishing to risk an armed conflict at this time, retreated to the mouth of the Tippecanoe River, a tributary of the Wabash. There, in 1808, they established the headquarters settlement of Tippecanoe. It soon became known as Prophet's Town, home to more than 1,000 Shawnees, Delawares, Wyandots, Ottawas, Ojibwas, and Kickapoos. It was a farming village. No liquor was allowed and traditional methods of Indian life were followed.

In November 1811 while Tecumseh was working with the Creeks, Choctaws, and Chickasaws in the southeast, Harrison moved a force of 900-1,000 men to the outskirts of Tippecanoe. While circumstances of the first provocation are unclear, on November 7, 1811 a battle began. While both sides sustained heavy injuries, Tenskwatawa was forced to retreat and the village was burned. Harrison gained national recognition which aided his 1840 election to the Presidency with the slogan, 'Tippecanoe and Tyler, too!'. The defeated Indians were shamed and disillusioned. Tecumseh, returning to find all hopes of an Indian union crushed, was furious that his brother had allowed the battle to be joined.

Tenskwatawa spent the rest of his life faced with the discredit of Tippecanoe. He lived in Canada until 1826 when he returned to his tribe, later moving to the vicinity of Cape Girardeau, Missouri, and to Wyandotte County, Kansas. In 1832 he was interviewed and painted by George Catlin, the well-known painter of Indian portraits and landscapes.

TEOSKAHATAY (Mdewakanton; fl. 17th century), traveled to Montreal in 1695 to reaffirm the friendship of the Sioux tribes for the French. He agreed to a treaty assuring safe travel to French trappers and explorers using the Saint Croix route to the Mississippi River. Teoskahatay never returned to his tribe, however; he died during his stay in Montreal.

TEZOZÓMOC (Tepanec; fl. 14th and 15th century), was the ruler of the Tepanecs for over 50 years, who created an empire, centered on his capital, Azcapotzalco, that dominated the Valley of Mexico and provided the nucleus for the later Aztec Empire.

Tezozómoc probably began his reign in 1371. Combining his shrewd diplomatic skill and the fighting ability of his vassals, especially the Mexica (later called Aztecs), he conquered a succession of cities, including Azcapotzalco's only rivals Xaltocan (1395) and Texcoco (1418). Once a city was conquered, Tezozómoc generally replaced its ruler with a relative, or, as in the case of Texcoco, which was given to the Mexica, gave it as a reward to a deserving vassal.

He also cemented his alliances with marriages of state, for example, giving Huitzilíhuitl (Mexica) a granddaughter to marry. In fact, the fight with Texcoco began because Ixtlilxóchitl, the new ruler, asserted his independence and rejected one of Tezozómoc's daughters for his wife.

Tezozómoc died in 1426 and the Tepanec Empire died with him because his heir was killed by a brother, Maxtla, who lasted two years before he lost it to the combined forces of Tenochtitlán, Texcoco, and Tlacopan (Tacuba), all former vassals or conquests of Tezozómoc.

THOMAS, ROBERT K. (Cherokee; 20th century), an anthropologist, is a founder and editor of *Indian Voices* (Chicago, 1963–68). A Cherokee, he has taught at Wayne State University in Detroit, Michigan.

THOMPSON, MORRIS (Athabascan; 20th century), became the youngest commissioner in the history of the Bureau of Indian Affairs when he assumed his post in December, 1973, at the age of 34. Born in Tanana, Alaska, he is descended from the Athabascans on his mother's side. He has worked as an electronics technical assistant with the National Aeronautics and Space Administration in Fairbanks, Alaska, and as an assistant to former Secretary of the Interior, Walter J. Hickel. He has served with the Bureau of Indian Affairs as the Alaska Area Director. Thompson was the first official commissioner of the Bureau since Louis Bruce resigned in December, 1972, following protracted demonstrations by militant Indians at the bureau's headquarters in Washington. Marvin Franklin acted unofficially as commissioner in the interim period, which witnessed the takeover of Wounded Knee, South Dakota, by Indians and the subsequent siege by the United States Government. At the time of his assuming office, Thompson, admitting that morale was low at the bureau, voiced plans to consult with Indians around the country on the future activities of the agency, and hoped in general to give Indians a sense that the BIA was concerned about their welfare.

THORPE, JAMES FRANCIS (Potawatomi; 1888–1953), whose Indian name was Mauch Chunk, was a United States athlete, considered one of the greatest athletes of all time.

Born near Prague, Oklahoma, of Irish, French and Indian descent, he was a star in both college and professional football. An All-American in 1911 and 1912, he was the star of Carlisle Institute in Pennsylvania. Representing the United States in the 1912 Olympic Games, he was the outstanding athlete in Stockholm, where he won both the decathlon (a ten-event competitive sport) and the pentathlon (five events). However, his gold medals were taken from him when it was discovered that he had innocently played some professional baseball in the summer of 1911, contrary to Olympic rules.

In addition to football, Thorpe was an outstanding baseball player, boxer, wrestler, swimmer, marksman, bowler, and golfer. He played baseball from 1913 to 1919 for such teams as the New York Giants and the Boston Braves. In the 1920s, he played professional football for the New York Giants and the Chicago Cardinals. In addition, in 1920 he became the first president of the American Professional Football Association. Voted the best athlete of the first half of the 20th century in an Associated Press Poll in 1950, Thorpe was named to both the College and Professional Football Hall of Fame.

TIKUMIGIZHIK (Chippewa; fl. 19th century), chief of the Chippewa at White Earth, fought with Hole-In-The-Day in 1862. Born at Gull Lake (circa 1830), Tikumigizhik moved to White Earth around 1868. The Indian Protestant preacher En-megahbowh converted the Chippewa chief to Christianity, and Tikumigizhik grew to be a wealthy and influential leader. Although he supported Hole-In-The-Day in the uprising of 1862, Tikumigizhik refused to take advantage of soldiers who were vulnerable to an onslaught. He explained that he held back when he thought of all the widows and orphans his followers would create.

TIMMONS, ALICE M. (Cherokee; August 10, 1914–   ), has been a librarian at the University of Oklahoma in Norman, Oklahoma. A Cherokee, she was born in Venita, Oklahoma. She has been active in community affairs.

TINKER, CLARENCE (Osage; November 21, 1887– June 7, 1942), a career Army officer who rose through the ranks to Major-General in the Army Air Corps was born near Edgin, Kansas. An Osage Indian, he entered the military in 1908, but his career took a decisive turn in 1920 when he enrolled in flying school. His rise to prominence paralleled the growing recognition of the importance of the air force. After the bombing of Pearl Harbor in December, 1941, Tinker, considered one of the Air Corp's ablest officers, was appointed commander of the Army Air Corps in Hawaii. On June 7, 1942, he was reported missing in action in the Battle of Midway. Tinker Air Force Base in Oklahoma City, Oklahoma, is named for him.

TÍZOC (Aztec; fl. late 15th century), seventh and least important Aztec *huey tlatoani* (chief speaker) who reigned without distinction from 1481 to 1486.

Tízoc was the grandson of two Aztec rulers, Itzcóatl (1426-40) and Moctezuma Ilhuicamina (1440-68), and the brother of his predecessor and successor, Axayácatl (1468-81) and Ahuítzotl (1486-1502). With such distinguished relatives he could have been expected to be an able ruler. However, he not only failed to add to the empire, but apparently fled from the field of battle, an act of great disgrace to the Aztecs.

Although he was something of a builder, having enlarged the temple to the gods Huitzilopochtli (war) and Tlaloc (rain) and perhaps other public buildings, his death was welcomed. Some accounts even say his own chiefs poisoned him because they were disgusted with his lack of military success, though this is probably exaggerated since the ruler's person was held in great awe.

TLACAÉLEL (Aztec; fl. 15th century), most important holder of the second highest Aztec office, *cihuacóatl* (woman snake), served as the principal advisor to three rulers, Itzcóatl (1426– 40), Moctezuma Ilhuicamina (1440– 68), and Axayácatl (1468– 81) and helped create the Aztec Empire.

Tlacaélel was a younger brother (or half-brother) of Moctezuma and they became Itzcóatl's military leaders, leading the Aztecs to victory over, and independence from, the Tepanecs in 1428.

During Moctezuma's reign, Tlacaélel held power almost equal to the ruler (only he and Moctezuma could wear shoes within the palace) and deserves much of the credit for that highly successful reign.

In fact, he has been called one of the three most important figures in the history of the Valley of Mexico. He, Moctezuma, and Nezahuacóyotl, the philosopher king of Texcoco, created the Aztec Empire out of city-states.

When Moctezuma made war the principal Aztec occupation by reserving privileges of nobility for those who fought, Tlacaélel worked to eliminate all worship of a comparatively gentle god, Quetzalcóatl, and to replace it with a warrior mysticism, complete with military orders, special privileges, and residences, more attune to the times.

Late in Moctezuma's reign, Tlacaélel's statue (and that of the ruler) was carved on Chapultepec and when Moctezuma died, in 1468, Tlacaélel was offered the throne by the council of nobles that selected Aztec rulers. He declined because of his age and probably died early in the reign of Axayácatl, who was chosen in his stead.

TLOTZIN (Acolhua; fl. 13th century), also spelled Tlohtzin, third ruler of the Acolhua at Coatlichan, on the eastern side of Lake Texcoco, in central Mexico, during the 13th century.

Tlotzin appears to have not been selected as ruler but to have moved away and established a new line of rulers from which the great ruler, Quinatzin, probably came.

TOMAS, JUAN (Seri; ?–1936), a war chief of the Seri Indians of northwestern Mexico, was well-known in the 1930s to U.S. scholars; he died boasting of the Seri reputation as the last warring tribe in the northern hemisphere.

In 1932 Juan Tomas claimed to be 103 years old; like many of his statements this must be considered an exaggeration. He was of the mainland Seri, who lived west of Hermosillo city, but he resettled on Tiburón island, in Kino Bay, to assume his title. In fact, the Tiburón Seris themselves did not consider

Juan Tomas a chief; his recognition came from the government of Sonora state after he signed a peace treaty in 1911. In the 1930s the U.S. authors Dane and Mary Coolidge visited Tiburón, where they recorded many of the stories and songs of the illiterate but crafty old chief. In 1936 Juan Tomas had an interview with the journalist Gordon Gordon, in which he said that the Seris had taken a vow of tribal suicide, as an alternative to accepting white civilization. He told Gordon a fantastic story of a secret temple of skulls, taken from white victims, where the Seris met to vow death to the white race. Shortly after this, Juan Tomas himself died of pneumonia, and was succeeded by Chico Romero.

Juan Tomas was not important as a leader or activist; his significance lay in his willingness to talk to the outside world, however unreliable his stories may have been.

TOMAU (Menominee; *c.* 1752–1818), properly known as Thomas Carron, was a Menominee chief of the Prairie-Chicken branch in Michigan who fought for the British during the War of 1812. Tribal chief by virtue of his authority and not by actual inheritance, Tomau was the son of the part French part Menominee chief Old Carron and an Abnaki woman. In 1805 Tomau was a guide for Zebulon Pike who was exploring the upper Mississippi River region of the Louisiana Purchase in an attempt to find the source of the river. In reports to the government, Pike spoke of Tomau's friendship for the U.S. When Tecumseh visited the Menominee before the War of 1812, Tomau refused to support Tecumseh's plans. Tomau spoke firmly of the need to maintain peace, but did permit those few among his warriors who disagreed with him to follow Tecumseh. Although Tomau wished to maintain neutrality, encroachments and attacks by whites and further urging by Tecumseh and the British convinced him of the necessity to join in the hostilities against the United States. Like many other chiefs of the Northwest tribes, Tomau was forced into the war.

Tomau immediately allied himself with Lt. Col. Alexander Dickson and, without fighting, took Mackinaw, Michigan on July 17, 1812. In 1813 he accompanied Dickson and Gen. Henry Procter in attacking Fort Sandusky, Ohio, and in 1814 once more with Dickson he defeated an American force at Mackinaw, Michigan. In 1816, after the defeat of the British and Indian forces, Tomau entered into treaty negotiations with the U.S. and allowed the construction of a U.S. fort on Menominee land. Another victim of excessive drinking, Tomau died in 1818 and was buried in Mackinaw.

TOMMANEY, THOMAS (Creek; June 12, 1913–   ), has held various positions in the field of education with the Bureau of Indian Affairs. A Creek, he was born in Eufaula, Oklahoma. He began his career with the bureau in 1938. He served as superintendent at the Haskell Institute in Lawrence, Kansas, and later as Assistant Area Director for the BIA in Oklahoma.

TOMOCHICHI (Creek; ?– October 5, 1739),was a Creek chief who played an important role in formulating the Creek relationship to the early British settlers. There are several variant spellings to his name; Thamachaychee, Tamachachi, and Tomeychee are the most common. He first came to notice as one of the signers of a treaty with the Carolina government in 1721. He was representing the lower Creek town of Apalachukla.

For reasons that are unclear, he was ostracized from his tribe shortly after 1721. He gained from the South Carolina government the right to settle near present-day Savannah, Georgia. There with a band of about 200 of his people he established the town of Yamacraw.

Upon the arrival of James Oglethorpe and founding of the colony of Georgia in 1733 Tomochichi established himself as a representative of the Creek nation. His initial attitude toward the settlers was friendly and under his auspices a treaty was concluded between the colony and the lower Creeks in 1733.

His success as a diplomat may have been the reason for the reconciliation which occurred between the upper and lower Creeks shortly after the Oglethorpe arrival. He was allowed to return to the main Creek towns to bring his family and friends back to Yamacraw.

His friendliness with the colonists gave him and his family the opportunity to go to England. Upon his return he continued to have peaceful relations with the British settlers until his death.

TOOANTUH was a famed athlete and respected person among 18th century Cherokees. He was born in approximately 1754 near Lookout Mountain, Tennessee. Although not a chief, his opinions and peacemaking efforts had great influence on the Cherokee people. An advocate of peace that he was, he often led war parties against other tribes who harassed his people. In 1818 after a raid on Cherokee towns by Osage tribesmen, Tooantuh or a member of the war council led a party of Cherokees who destroyed an Osage village. Eighty people were killed or captured. He participated in the Cherokee-Creek war in 1812–14, serving under Andrew Jackson at the battle of Emuckfaw and Horseshoe Bend. He was well known for his bravery.

His reputation as an athlete came from his skill as a ball player. Such games were important entertainments in Cherokee society and status was the reward for expertise.

He was removed in 1838, along with the majority of Cherokee, to Indian territory. There he was one of the first to take up farming. He was known to his people as Dustu, meaning Spring Frog.

TOPENEBEE was an early 19th century southern Michigan Potawatomi chief who became one of Tecumseh's war chiefs during the War of 1812. On August 3, 1795, Topenebee, on behalf of the Potawatomi, signed the Treaty of Greenville, Ohio, resulting from the victory of Gen. Anthony Wayne at Fallen Timbers, which opened the Ohio region to white settlement. From 1795 on he signed a number of treaties giving access and ceding land to the U.S.

In 1810 Tecumseh travelled to Topenebee's village to persuade him to join his confederacy to halt the white settlers. Topenebee was reluctant even though his warriors gave Tecumseh their overwhelming support. Tecumseh skillfully applied pressure. Topenebee already had signed away so much land through treaties that he could not expect to avoid being caught up in the coming hostilities. Becoming a strong supporter of The Prophet's teachings, he joined Tecumseh and commanded several other Potawatomi chiefs.

In July of 1812, Topenebee joined the chiefs who travelled with Tecumseh to Fort Malden where they announced their allegiance to the British. He took a leading part in the August 15, 1812 massacre of Fort Dearborn (Chicago), but tried to stem the unnecessary slaughter that occured. He was present at the Battle of the Thames River where Indian resistance was finally broken.

After the War of 1812, like many other chiefs, he became a supporter of peace with the U.S. Topenebee offered no aid before or during Black Hawk's 1832 uprising, and maintained his neutrality. During his life he signed 12 different treaties including on October 27, 1832 treaty which ceded tribal lands in southern Michigan to the U.S., and the September 26, 1833 treaty at Chicago under which the majority of the Potawatomi were to remove west. Topenebee and a number of other chiefs managed to exclude themselves from the final Potawatomi removal in 1838 which was accompanied by incredible suffering and death.

TOPÍLTZIN (Toltec; fl. 10th century), was also called Quetzalcóatl, ruler and founder of the Toltec Empire and its capital, Tollán (Tula), whose life is so enmeshed in legend it is impossible to narrate with confidence.

Most sources place him in the 10th century but some list two Toltec rulers with this name. To confuse matters more, the sources do not agree on the names or order of rule for Toltec rulers, some calling Topíltzin the ninth ruler and others the fourth and fifth rulers.

The noted Aztec scholar, George C. Vaillant, believed the account in the *Anales de Cuanhtitlan* (also called the *Codex Chimalpopoca*) best matched archaeological evidence. According to that source, Topíltzin was the posthumous son of Mixcóatl or (Totepeuh), the chief of a Nahua-speaking people who settled at Culhuacán (now in Mexico City). Topíltzin's uncle, Ilhuitimal, murdered Mixcóatl, succeeded him, and Topíltzin was raised by priests of Quetzalcóatl at Xochicalco (now in Morelos).

When Topíltzin attained manhood, he returned to Culhuacán and avenged his father by killing Ilhuitimal. He then moved to Tollán (probably Tula, in Hidalgo, north of Mexico City) in about 968, where he founded the Toltec Empire, taking the name Quetzalcóatl from the god he served.

A quarrel over religious practices resulted in his exile from Tollán and he went to Maya country, to the east, probably in about 987, although dating his life is risky.

Whatever the facts of his life, to the Aztecs, whose legends and historical poems began with his reign and sought to show a direct Aztec descent from him and the Toltecs, he was an heroic figure with a reign of peace and culture.

Other accounts say he was the high priest of Quetzalcóatl who got into conflict with the supporters of another god, Tezcatlipoca, and was forced from Tollán. Some versions have him sailing from about Vera Cruz into the east and a legend that he would return one day to reestablish his rule, sprang up. Supposedly, Hernán Cortés fulfilled this prophecy when he landed at Vera Cruz because he had the fair skin, beard, and helmet associated with the god.

Finally, 987 is also the traditional Maya date for the arrival of Kukulcán, a man who came from the west, took over the Yucatán, and established his capital at Chichén Itzá. Kukulcán, means "feathered serpent" which is also the translation of Quetzalcóatl, thus linking Topíltzin to the whole body of Yucatán Maya legend.

TORIN (Yaqui; fl. 1925), was a Yaqui Indian chief who, along with his allies was killed by a Mexican army detachment in the command of a General Zertache. 1927 was the last year of concerted Yaqui violence in Mexico's Sonora state.

TOTEPEUH (Toltec; fl. 9th century), was king of Tula (Tollán), Central Mexico, is credited with construction of two majestic temples, to the Sun and Moon. Fourth of his line, he retired in accordance with Toltec custom after ruling 52 years, possibly in AD 875. The temple ruins still stand as the famous Pyramids of Teotihuacán.

TOTOPOTOMOI (Pamunkey; *c.* 1627–1656), chief of the Pamunkey Indians, fought and died in a bloody engagement along the James River, while aiding the colonial government of Virginia defend itself against invading inland mountain tribes. Totopotomoi had been second in succession from Opechancanough to inherit the leadership of the Powhatan confederacy prior to the English destroying that tribal union in 1644. Twelve years later, however, he and nearly 100 Pamunkey warriors joined with colonial troops to repel an invasion of inland mountain tribes. Totopotomoi and nearly all of the Pamunkey warriors were killed in the clash, as the Virginians were routed in a disastrous defeat.

Totopotomoi's widow, called Queen Anne by the English, then became chief of the Pamunkey.

TSHISHAT (Makah) was chief of his people.

TUBANAMA (Tubanama; fl. 16th century), was chief of a tribe of Indians of the Darien Mountains, lower Panama, and one of the wealthiest chiefs of the area during the time of the Spanish conquest. The Indian allies of Balboa, particularly the chief Comagre and his son Panquiaco, told the Spanish of Tubanama's reputation for inhuman cruelty and his rich gold holdings. In late 1513, Balboa marched with a force of 190 men, and fell on Tubanama by night. As was his custom, Balboa spared the chief's life, hoping to gain not only his friendship but the secret of his gold. In 1515, Tubanama was attacked by the Spanish lieutenant Juan de Ayora, but the Indian chief successfully resisted the invasion. Nevertheless, the Spanish established a post used in their passages across the Isthmus. The Spanish named Tubanama's tribe after their chief.

TUCKER, CHARLES (Shawnee).

TUHOCEE, MATHLA (Seminole; fl. early 19th century), or Tuckose Emathla was a Seminole chief. The first chief of a united Seminole nation, he was known to whites as John Hicks. His Indian name meant mole or ant leader. Before being chosen as chief of all the Seminoles, he had succeeded Neamathla as chief of the Seminole lands west of the Suwanne River in Florida. Mathla himself resided in the town of Mikasuki. Mathla Tuhocee's election as chief of all Seminoles was engineered by white officers in Florida. The Seminoles functioned successfully in small bands and without centralized leadership. Whites, however, found it convenient to have a single representative with whom they could deal.

Mathla was a member of a contingent of prominent Seminoles sent to inspect western lands proposed for settlement. Members of the delegation, including Hicks signed a document stating they were satisfied with the land. Later this document was repudiated by the Seminoles. Mathla died in approximately 1833.

TUSKATCHE MICO (Creek) was the king of the Cusitahs.

TUSTENNUGGEE, EMALTHA was a Creek chief. Born in approximately 1793 near the Tallapoosa River he was known as *Jim Boy*. He was a leader before and during the removal in 1838. He was a follower of William MacIntosh, a pro-American chief who signed the 1825 treaty with the U.S. ceding Creek lands.

In 1838 he joined the U.S. in its fight to remove the Seminoles from Florida. His promise to fight the Seminoles was based upon a return promise from the U.S. that his family would not be removed to Indian territory and his property would be left intact until he returned.

He raised a band of 700 warriors and fought courageously, if unsuccessfully. At one point he attempted to arrange a truce between the U.S. and the Seminoles. Upon his return to the Creek nation he found that the U.S. government had broken its promises to him. His family had been removed and his property occupied by white settlers. He left the Creek homeland to join his family only to hear that they had drowned when the steamboat in which they were traveling sank. His later career is unknown.

TZIKALTZA (Nez Percé) was the son of Clark of the Lewis and Clark Expedition 1804-6.

□ □ □

Tahchee

Talkhorse

Tallchief, Maria

Tallchief, Marjorie

Tendoy

Tenskwatawa

Thompson, Morris

Tomochichi

Tooantuh

Tshishat

Tucker, Charles

Tuskatche Mico

Tustennuggee, Emathla

Tzikaltza

U

UNCAS (Mohegan; ?– 1682 or 1683), Chief of the Mohegan, played an important role in the Indian history of colonial southern New England. As a subchief under Pequot Chief Sachem Sassacus, Uncas rebelled and with a band of followers settled on the west bank of the Pequot (Thames) river about three miles south of the present Norwich, Connecticut. This group known as *Mohegan* is mentioned as a *tribe* in early records beginning about 1636. Uncas and the Mohegan supported the English in the Pequot war (1636); King Philip's war (1675); and through the Revolutionary Period. Uncas was noted for his strategy and cunning in warfare; a faithful friend; and relentless toward his enemies. Uncas, wiley strategist that he was, saw that it was to his advantage to support the English and adopt their ways as a means of survival for his people. For this stand he was condemned by many and lauded by others.

Uncas *Fox*, (literally *the circler*) was the older of two sons of Oweneco and Meekun-ump. His brother was named Waweequa. References to the early life of Uncas are lacking. As for tribal affiliations it appears that the Mohegan (Mohican *Wolf people*) migrated from the upper Hudson river valley in the early 1600's to the present Connecticut and parts of eastern New York and western Massachusetts. Local tribes called them *pequataug* meaning destroyers or invaders hence the name Mohegan Pequot. The Mohican (Mohegan, Mahikan) were related to the northern or "Wolf" division of the Delawares or Lenni-Lenape.

According to Delaware tradition "Some of the Wolves went east" and the Connecticut Mohegan always maintained that "Our people came from the northwest" indicating the area in eastern New York state and northwestern Massachusetts. The group finally settled around New London and Groton, Connecticut and were generally known as *Pequot*.

Uncas

In 1626, Uncas married the daughter of Sassacus, Grand Sachem of the Pequot. Claiming to be a distant cousin of Sassacus this union made him more closely connected with the *Royal Family*, and he felt that he should be granted more authority within the tribe. Continuing unrest resulted in Uncas and a band of followers withdrawing and settling on the west bank of the Pequot (Thames) river. This group known as *Mohegan* is mentioned in Colonial records beginning about 1636. Uncas and the Mohegan were friendly toward the Colonists much to the displeasure of the Pequot and other local Indian leaders in the area. Uncas realized that with a small band of less than a hundred the white man would soon dominate, not only the Mohegan, but other small tribes in the area so it was to his advantage to adopt the ways of the colonists. Trouble was brewing within the Pequot and English villages and following acts of hostilities against the English, the Pequot became involved in a war with the colonists in 1637. Uncas assisted Roger Williams in securing the aid of Indian allies in joining an attack on the Pequot Fort at Mystic which resulted in their annihilation. An estimated 700 men, women and children were believed to have been within the village and only a few escaped. English losses were light — some twenty wounded and two killed.

Survivors sought refuge with other Indians; Sassacus fled to the Mohawk where he was slain. With the death of Sassacus and the Pequot no longer an existing power in Indian affairs Uncas was in control of the remaining Indian tribes throughout Connecticut. There was more trouble ahead for Uncas and the Mohegan when word was received that Chief Miantonomoh and the Narragansett were planning to attack the Mohegan village. Rivalry between the Mohegan and Narragansett chiefs had existed for a long time and in 1643 the battle was on at the *Great Plain* in Mohegan territory outside the present Norwich, Connecticut. The Mohegan scouts informed Uncas of the approaching

Narragansett chief and his warriors. Estimates of numbers vary. It seems likely that the Narragansett numbered around 500 and the Mohegan not more than 200. Uncas sent one of his men to ask Miantonomoh if he would agree to the two chiefs meeting man to man to settle their grievances. The offer was rejected. Miantonomoh said "My men came to fight and fight they will." Uncas had told the Mohegan men that if his offer was rejected that he would fall on his face as a signal for them to charge the enemy. Upon receiving the negative reply, Uncas fell on his face and the Mohegan put the Narragansett to flight, many losing their lives as they attempted to leap over the falls of the Yantic river. Miantonomoh was pursued by a Mohegan, Tantaquiesen (Tantaquidgeon) an aide to Uncas who was "the first to lay hands on the enemy chief". This enabled Chief Uncas to have the honor of capturing Miantonomoh. Traditionally "A Chief must take a Chief" thus Tantaquidgeon being of lesser rank could not have the honor.

This has been referred to "As the most purely Indian battle in the annals of New England." Only bows and arrows and clubs were used and the English were not directly concerned.

Miantonomoh was taken to the Fort of Uncas and a meeting was arranged with the Commissioners at Hartford, Connecticut, to discuss the fate of the captive. Uncas was told that he could use his judgement as to the means of disposing of his captive but it must be carried out beyond the boundaries of Hartford — in other words, in Mohegan territory. Miantonomoh was slain by Uncas' brother, Waweequa.

Angered by the capture and death of their chief at the hands of Uncas, the Narragansett besieged the Mohegan village at Fort Shantok in 1645. Food supplies were low and Uncas sent a scout to Saybrook, the nearest English settlement, to tell them of the plight of the Mohegan. In response to Uncas' plea for aid, beef, beans, and corn were brought by boat up the Pequot (Thames) river and smuggled into the Fort under cover of darkness. At daybreak, the Mohegan hoisted a piece of beef on a pole outside the Fort. Seeing the beef and some Englishmen in the area, the Narragansett left the scene.

In 1765, Uncas and a few Mohegan men joined the English in the struggle known as King Philip's War which lasted most of the year. None of the battles were fought on Connecticut soil but Connecticut tribes were involved — some with the Indians; others with the English. This proved to have been the last open warfare between the Indian tribes of southern New England and the colonists.

Through the years, Uncas and his sons, Oweneco and Attawanhood (Joshua) had deeded many acres of Mohegan land to their English friends for favors accorded them during times of warfare. Uncas and the few surviving Mohegan continued to live on the old hunting grounds with more and more non-Indians taking up residence among them. Uncas finally retired to his wigwam at a place called *Uncas Hill* in Mohegan, Montville township, Connecticut. There he died *at a great age* in 1682 or '83. At the top of Mohegan Hill, Connecticut Route 32 is a marker erected by the State, *Mohegan: Seat of Uncas— Friend of the English*. Here live 35 of a known 200 descendants of the Mohegan on land that is individually owned. The reservation system was terminated in 1860 at the request of Mohegan leaders.

Near by, is a small Indian museum owned and operated by Chief Harold Tantaquidgeon X and his sister, Gladys Tantaquidgeon, tenth generation descendants of Chief Uncas. The museum is dedicated to the perpetuation of the history and traditions of the Mohegan and other New England Indians.

UNSORIUNT (Cayuse) also called *Billy Joshua* was born in 1858.

URRACA (Guaymí; fl. early 16th century), was the Guaymí Indian chief who ruled the Veraguas region of Panama, as early as 1514 and began a concerted resistance to the Spanish conquest of the Isthmus. In 1521 Urraca razed Natá, the first Spanish settlement on Panama's southern coast. Natá's founder, Gaspar de Espinosa, sought vengeance on Urraca, but the resourceful chief ambushed Espinosa's expedition, which was saved only by the arrival of a cavalry force. In 1522, with the Spanish firmly entrenched in neighboring Chiriquí, Urraca threatened to attack, but he was deceived by a Spanish offer of peace. The chief was captured, but managed to escape. After a protracted war, Urraca was deserted by his followers, and died in 1531.

Unsoriunt

V

VANN, DAVID (Cherokee; fl. 19th century), was a Cherokee chief who prior to his removal had been conciliatory to the U.S., signing a land cession treaty in 1806. During and after the removal he aligned himself with chief John Ross who fought removal. In the new Cherokee nation he assisted Ross in creating a peace between the Ross faction and those who had signed the New Echota treaty. He encouraged education in the new nation and helped to establish the Cherokee female seminary.

VICTORIO (Apache; ?-October, 1880), was one of the most feared leaders in the war of vengence designed to drive all white men from Apacheria.

Inspired by the great Mimbreño Mangas Coloradas, Victorio resisted efforts by U.S. officials to negotiate a peace program. The Apache had witenssed too many of their leaders murdered under a flag of truce, but in 1865, destitute and tired of war, he did consent to visit Basque Redondo Reservation, in New Mexico, where, he was assured, his people would receive rations and protection. He failed to show, whereupon Capt. N.H. Davis decreed that every male Indian be killed without mercy. The situation in the Southwest became desperate, with the Apache as much victim as victimized.

The Warm Springs Reservation in New Mexico had become a haven for many of the renegades, among them Victorio. At that agency, noted for its corruption, raiders could rest while trading their plunder for whiskey and supplies. In 1877 Indian agent John Philip Clum was ordered to arrest the renegades at Warm Springs and take them to San Carlos. Victorio agreed to go, but only because he knew that to resist was tantamount to death. At the despised San Carlos Reservation he bided his time until September, then taking more than 300 men, women, and children, he bolted, intending to go to Mexico. But pursuing troops forced him south, and he surrendered his dwindling band at Fort Wingate, a Navajo reservation. Since official Washington could not agree on a proper solution to the problem, the renegades were sent back to Warm Springs, closely guarded for a year, at War Department expense. When Gen. William T. Sherman threatened to release the band, the Indian Bureau decided to send the prisoners to San Carlos.

Victorio's people had led a quiet and productive life at Warm Springs. Now they were told that they must abandon their farms and the houses they had built because Warm Springs was to be restored to the public domain. In utter disbelief Victorio explained that this was his people's beloved country; they had been born here and they had no intention of going to San Carlos. Before daybreak he and a hundred other warriors were gone. They spent the winter high in the mountains. In February, destitute once more, Victorio and 22 of his warriors rode into Warm Springs, asking only that they be allowed to remain at the post. The commanding officer's sympathetic agreement set off bitter dispute in Washington. In April Victorio was informed that he was to go to Mescalero Reservation, in New Mexico, where he promised to farm and remain at peace. His arrival struck terror to the hearts of citizens of the region, who immediately set in motion plans to destroy him. A grand jury indicted him for murder and theft of livestock. When news of the indictment reached Victorio, he flew into a rage, accusing the reservation agent of a doublecross. Frightened, the agent notified Fort Stanton that he needed protection, but when the troops arrived, Victorio had departed, taking with him 150 warriors.

Every military post in Apacheria was alerted that fall of 1879, and thus began a trail of burning, plundering, and killing, of hide and seek, involving Indians and soldiers, white citizens, women and children, before Victorio vanished into Mexico. Reinforced by irregulars, civilians, and Indian scouts, more than a thousand American cavalry took up the chase in January. Repeatedly, Victorio eluded his pursurers or succeeded in annihilating them. In May H.K. Parker, chief of Indian scouts, picked up Victorio's trail and trapped him on the Palomas River. Short on ammunition and rations, the scout sent a messenger to Gen. Edward Hatch, asking for reinforcements. None came, and, certain that the messenger had failed to get through, Parker went back to Ojo Caliente. Instead of sending help, Hatch had ridden to Santa Fe to telegraph headquarters that he had Victorio trapped and would wipe out his band. Some of Hatch's men openly denounced him as an imbecile.

Fighting continued, with the Mexican government offering $3,000 for Victorio's head. The U.S. Cavalry was permitted to join in the hunt for him under Mexican Gen. Joaquin Terrazas. Just when capture seemed imminent, the Mexican government ordered U.S. troops to leave the country.

In October, General Terrazas' men surrounded Victorio's band, which was almost without ammunition. Victorio and 60 warriors were killed. Some women and children were also killed; 68 were captured, but 30 men escaped the trap to continue the bloody war for another six years.

VIZENOR, GERALD ROBERT (Ojibwa; October 22, 1934), a poet, professor, and guidance director, is an Ojibway, member of the Minnesota Chippewa Tribe. He was born in Minneapolis, Minnesota. After working for several correctional agencies in Minnesota he entered graduate school at the University of Minnesota. Later he joined the faculty of the Department of Indian Studies at Bemidji State College in Bemidji, Minnesota. Among his published works of poetry are *Seventeen Chirps* (1964) and *Empty Swings* (1967).

Victorio

W

WABAN (Nipmuc; ?– *c.* 1677), was a 17th century *praying Indian* of the Nipmuc people, a friend of missionary John Eliot and a leader of the Christian converts among the Indians.

Waban was probably born in the first decade of the 17th century at Musketaquid (now Concord, Mass.). He was living at Nonantum (now Newton) in 1646, when he welcomed John Eliot to his wigwam. He was described by Eliot as a *chief minister of justice* at that time. Eliot conducted his first service in the Algonquian language at Nonantum and returned there regularly to preach.

Waban requested of Eliot land on which to build a town, and this Eliot obtained from the General Court of Massachusetts. When the new town was established at Natick in 1651, Waban was its town clerk. At Eliot's recommendation, the government of the town followed the Biblical pattern of a hierarchy of one ruler of one hundred, two rulers of fifty, and ten rulers of ten. Waban was chosen as a ruler of fifty. He was later the justice of the peace, and in 1670 he was said to be the chief ruler of this community of Christian Indians (which four years later numbered 29 families, or about 145 persons).

Shortly before the outbreak of King Philip's War in 1675, Waban learned of the impending Indian attack and warned the English. However, the whites suspected the Christian Indians of duplicity, and Waban was among many sent as prisoners to Deer Island later that year. He was among the sick who were returned in 1676. He probably died about 1677.

Waban encouraged many other Indians to accept Christianity. Daniel Gookin described him as "a person of great prudence and piety." Eliot stated that Waban's gift lay in "ruling, judging of cases, wherein he is patient, constant, and prudent, insomuch that he is respected among them, for they have chosen him a ruler of fifty, and he ruleth well according to his measure."

WABANAQUOT (Ojibwa; fl. 19th century), also White Cloud was the principal chief of the Chippewa bands living along the Mississippi River. Wabanaquot was not born into a long line of hereditary chiefs; his father had been appointed chief by a U.S. Indian agent who felt that Wabojeeg (Wabanaquot's father) would prove conciliatory. Wabanaquot, nonetheless, succeeded as chief upon his father's death.

Wabanaquot drank heavily and — while under the influence — plotted against the government Indian agents. In fact, Wabanaquot hurt his own people by his hostility to three agents who were sincerely trying to aid the Chippewa. The chief moved his band to the White Earth Reservation in 1868, where in 1871 he converted to Christianity. He persisted in his drinking habit, though, until his death. Despite his many vices and undistinguished record of achievement, Wabanaquot was honored posthumously with a monument from the State of Minnesota placed over his grave.

WABOKIESHIEK (Winnebago-Sauk; c. 1794–1841), known as White Cloud and also called the Prophet, born on the Rock River, Illinois, was a half Winnebago, half Sauk medicine man and prophet who advised Black Hawk in his unsuccessful uprising of 1832. Neapope, Black Hawk's assistant, having discussed Indian land rights along the Rock River with the British, informed Wabokieshiek of Black Hawk's proposed Indian confederacy to oust the whites. In a trance Wabokieshiek revealed that a great army would rise up behind Black Hawk, and would fight to victory over the whites. Neapope told this to Black Hawk, and falsely informed him that he would have British military support. Black Hawk was convinced that success was inevitable.

Wabokieshiek advised Black Hawk throughout the hostilities and was with him at the defeat at the mouth of the Bad Axe River. They escaped in an attempt to reach Prairie La Crosse, Wisconsin and cross the Mississippi River, but were captured by Winnebago Indians. He and Black Hawk were sent to Washington (April, 1833). They thought they were going as visitors, but after seeing President Andrew Jackson they were incarcerated at Fort Monroe, Virginia until released on June 4. On their return trip through several east coast cities, Wabokieshiek spoke publicly professing his desire for peace in the future. Disgraced as a prophet, he lived quietly among the Sauk and Fox, and died among the Winnebago.

Wabokieshiek cultivated an extreme hostility toward the U.S., and yet often fed whites travelling near his village. As a medicine man he exerted great influence over his Winnebago and Sauk followers, and especially over his long time friend Black Hawk. Keokuk rightly maintained that without Wabokieshiek's influence there might not have been an uprising in 1832.

WADLEY, MARIE LUCILLE (Cherokee-Shawnee; December 16, 1906–   ), is noted for her work as tribal operations officer in the Muskogee Area Office of the Bureau of Indian Affairs. Of Cherokee-Shawnee descent she was born in Pensacola, Oklahoma. She joined the bureau in 1925 and has written a number of articles on Indian topics.

WAFFORD, JAMES D. (Cherokee; 1806–1896) was a Cherokee translator. Called Tsuskwanunnawta (worn-out blanket) by his people, he was born in 1806 near present day Clarkesville, Georgia. He was a half-breed Cherokee whose paternal grandfather was an officer in the American army during the Revolution and who established the controversial *Wafford Settlement* on Cherokee land.

The land was not officially acquired by the settlers until 1804. Wafford's mother was a cousin of Sequoya.

Shortly before Sequoya completed the first written Cherokee alphabet, Wafford had translated a Sunday School speller into phonetic Cherokee. In 1824 he was a census enumerator for a district of the Eastern Cherokee nation. It was during this time that he learned much of the Cherokee folklore he was later to transmit to the Bureau of American Ethnology.

During the removal of Cherokees from their lands to Indian territory in 1838 Wafford was a commander of the largest group of emigrants. He was a member of the National Cherokee Council.

He died in 1896 in the eastern part of the Cherokee nation in what is now Oklahoma.

WAHSHUNGAH (Kansa) was chief in the 1880s.

WAKEMAN, RICHARD K. (Santee; February 9, 1923—   ), has served as a tribal officer of the Flandreau Santee Sioux. Born in Flandreau, South Dakota, he was in the United States Marines during World War II and in the Army during the Korean War. He has been active in Indian affairs in South Dakota.

WALKINGSTICK, HOWARD CHANDLER (Cherokee; January 7, 1915—   ), works as a social welfare consultant and specialist in service training for the Department of Institutions Social and Rehabilative Services in Oklahoma City, Oklahoma. A Cherokee Indian, he was born in Tahlequah, Oklahoma. He earned a Masters in Social Work from the University of Denver in 1949 and served as a director with the Bureau of Indian Affairs from 1935–70, receiving the Distinguished Service Award of the Department of the Interior in 1967.

WALKS IN THE WATER (Blackfoot) was the wife of Little Dog.

WALLACE, AMOS LEWIS (Inuit; November 28, 1920–   ), is an Inuit craftsman who was born in Juneau, Alaska. Still living in Juneau, he is a member and past-president of the Alaska Native Brotherhood. He is known for his fine, hand-carved totems, which are on display in museums across the United States and in the Indian Village in Disneyland.

WALLACE, GLADYS DYKE (Peoria; 20th century), a prominent Tulsa, Oklahoma stockbroker, is the daughter of a chief of the Peoria Indians and was born in Commerce, Oklahoma. Educated at the Haskell Institute, she received the Outstanding Graduate Award in 1970. In the 1950s she left her career as an executive secretary to work as a securities dealer and is a registered representative of the New York Stock Exchange.

WALZ, ERMA HICKS (Cherokee; October 10, 1915–   ), retired December 31, 1970, from the position of Chief, Division of Tribal Operations, Bureau of Indian Affairs, Washington, D. C.

She was born in Hulbert (Cherokee County), Oklahoma, to Owen and Etta McDaniel Hicks. Both her parents are enrolled members of the Cherokee Tribe of Oklahoma, and she is one-fourth degree Cherokee Indian.

She was graduated from the business school of Haskell Institute, Lawrence, Kansas, in June 1935. In September of that year, she joined the staff of the Bureau of Indian Affairs in Washington, D.C., as junior stenographer.

In 1936, Mrs. Walz continued her education by enrolling in evening classes at George Washington University, and subsequently attended evening classes at the University of Illinois and Northwestern University after the Bureau of Indian Af-

fairs moved its central offices to Chicago during
World War II. At Northwestern, her undergraduate
studies emphasized her personal and professional
interest in government and public administration.

From 1938, her work in the Bureau of Indian
Affairs gave her increasing responsibilities in the
areas of tribal organization and government. This
involved such activities as giving technical advice
and assistance to Indian tribes in developing and
writing their constitutions, by-laws, charters
and amendments; assisting in matters relating to
tribal elections and tribal budgets; helping in the
preparation of tribal rolls; and doing research to
determine the proper beneficiaries of claims awards
to Indian tribes, and drafting proposed legislation to
authorize the disposition of the awards. Mrs. Walz
held virtually every key position within the Division of Tribal Operations.

She was named Chief of the Division of Tribal
Operations in 1965.

Mrs. Walz attended the first conference held for
the purpose of organizing the National Congress of
American Indians, and was elected as secretary of
the conference. She was a charter member of the
NCAI.

She was honored by being named "Boss of the
Year," in 1969, by the L'Enfant Chapter of the
American Business Women's Association in Wash-
ington, D. C.

She is married to Peter F. Walz who is of Chippewa Indian descent and is retired from the Bureau
of Indian Affairs after more than 35 years service.

WAMDITANKA (Dakota; 1827– *c.* 1900), also Big
Eagle or Jerome Big Eagle reluctantly participated
in the Sioux uprising of 1862, but he did what he
could to prevent the killing of innocent whites and
mixed bloods. An accomplished warrior, Wamditanka often wore a headdress with six feathers to
show that he had taken six Chippewa scalps during
tribal warfare. He succeeded his father, Gray Iron,

as chief of a band of 150 to 200 Mdewakanton Sioux living in a Minnesota village near Crow Creek. In 1862, his warriors pressured Wamditanka to join the Sioux uprising, and the chief submitted; but he did not take part in the massacres of settlers, and actually used his influence to save lives when he could. Following the battle of Birch Coolie in 1862, Wamditanka surrendered, whereupon he was tried, convicted, and sent to prison for three years as punishment for his participation in the uprising. When released, he converted to Christianity and lived out his years at Granite Falls, Minnesota.

WANETA (Dakota; *c.* 1795—1848), was a Yanktonai Sioux of the Pabaksa or Cuthead band, son of Shappa or Red Thunder. He enlisted with his father in the English service in the War of 1812, and fought valiantly at Ft. Meigs and Sandusky, winning his name by his bravery in charging the Americans in the open. After the war he was given a captain's commission by the British, and visited England. He continued to sympathize with the British until 1820, when he attempted to destroy Ft. Snelling. He afterward heartily supported American interests. Waneta was a dominant chief of the Sioux and exceedingly active in his operations. He signed the treaty of trade and intercourse at Ft. Pierre, July 5, 1825, and on Aug. 17 of the same year signed the treaty of Prairie du Chien which fixed the boundaries of the Sioux territory. His name is variously spelled, as Wahnaataa, Wanotan, and Wawnahton.

WAPASHA (Dakota; 1718—*c.* 1799), or Red Leaf was the name of a succession of chiefs of the Mdewakanton Sioux. The first Wapasha of which there is historical knowledge was born at the head of Rum River., Minn., in 1718. His father was a chief of the same name, and his mother a Chippewa captive. In 1747, through relatives of his mother, he negotiated peace between the Chippewa and his own people. About 1763 an English trader, known to the Indians as Mallard Duck, was killed at his store at St. Anthony's Falls by a Sioux named Ixatape, and in retaliation the English withdrew trade from the Sioux. By this time they had become so dependent on the traffic that destitution and suffering ensued, and Wapasha determined to take the murderer to Quebec and deliver him to the English. With a hundred of his tribesmen he started with Ixatape, but one by one the members of the party returned to the Mississippi; by the time Green Bay was reached few remained, and there Ixatape escaped; but undaunted, Wapasha with five others kept on, and, reaching Quebec, offered himself as a sacrifice for the sins of his people. His unselfish action made a deep impression upon the English, and he was accorded much honor.

He led the Sioux in a well-planned campaign in 1778 to drive back the Chippewa and recover the ancestral lands of the Sioux about Spirit Lake, Minn., but after some notable victories his party was ambushed. Two years later he was able to avenge his loss upon the Chippewa in a notable battle near Elk River. He served the English in the Revolution, and upon his visit to Mackinaw, Col. DePeyster, the commandant, dedicated a poem to him and made him the subject of a great ovation. He served in the West with Langlade, but his service was not of great importance. Before his death, he established his band at the site of Winona, Minn., at a village called Kiyudsa.

WAPASHA II (Dakota; 1769–1855), was a Mdewakanton Sioux who, like his father, sided with the British in the American Revolution and also in the War of 1812, after which he transferred his allegiance to the United States. He, too, stood well with the whites of his time. He was blind in one eye as a result of a childhood accident.

Lieutenant Zebulon M. Pike stopped for a council with Wapasha on his way up the Mississippi River in the fall of 1805. Major Thomas Forsyth came to his village near Winona in August 1819. "This man is no beggar," reported the Major, "nor does he drink."

Wapasha attended numerous councils in the interests of peace between tribes, although the results were less than successful, especially between the Sioux and the Chippewa. He died in a smallpox epidemic along with many others of his band.

WAPASHA III (Dakota; ?– April 23, 1876), known as Joseph Wapasha was a Mdewakanton Sioux, who wanted peace but saw no honorable way to achieve it for his people. Although well regarded, Wapasha was not as easily deceived as his good-natured grandfather or his father, whom he succeeded as chief of the Red Leaf band. Too many promises had been made and broken by ruthless white men in their time and his.

The treaty of Traverse des Sious (July 1851) called for cession by the upper Sioux of all their land claims in present Minnesota and part of South Dakota. The treaty of Mendota called for the lower bands, including Wapasha's to follow suit. He was one of the hold-outs. But already the region was overrun with settlers, and the Sioux were reservation Indians even though there were no specific sites set aside for them. Finally, government officials decided to locate an agency on the south side of the Minnesota River about 15 miles from Fort Ridgely. But as the years slipped by, annuities failed to arrive on time, if at all. Most of the Indians spent more time off the reservation than on, sometimes to hunt, but lack of wild game and the steady encroachment of squatters frustrated the effort of even the most competent Indian agents and the missionaries sent to Christianize and educate them in the white man's way.

Wapasha was among the delegates to Washington in June 1858. The treaties that evolved from four weeks of wrangling were even worse than previous documents. Most of the payments agreed upon went to the traders to settle debts contracted by the Indians simply because they had no other source for acquiring the necessities for survival. Indian hostility increased at an alarming pace.

Wapasha opposed war, but when it came in 1862, he was forced to side with the hostiles or abandon his chieftancy. While he was seen at various encounters, riding a splendid white horse, he was obviously a reluctant warrior. In fact, he did everything he could to protect white women and children. It was he who wrote a secret message to H. H. Sibley asking for surrender terms.

After the uprising he went with his people, first to a concentration camp on the Missouri, and finally to the Santee reservation in Nebraska, where he died. He was succeeded by his second son, Napolean Wapasha, but it was the end of the line for the great Wapasha dynasty.

WAPELLO (Fox; 1787– March 15, 1842), also spelled Wapella, Wapulla, Wapalaw, and Waupella, born at Prairie du Chien, Wisconsin, was the principal chief of the Fox nation and a friend of the U.S. government. His village, prior to 1829, was situated not far from Fort Armstrong and east of the Mississippi River. Although his early years as chief were not marked by any significant activity, when all Sauk and Fox lands in Wisconsin and Illinois were ceded to the U.S. in 1804 by a treaty signed by five Sauk and Fox chiefs in Washington, D.C. without authorization, he quietly moved.

Wapello had always been next in rank to Keokuk, supported his moved to become head chief of the Sauk nation, and generally agreed with Keokuk's attitude of compliance with the U.S. and with the provisions of the 1804 treaty. He took part in the subsequent negotiations concerning boundary definitions and final transfer of territories, and in 1829 removed his people to settle in a swampy area known as the Muscatine slough in Iowa.

Wapello was a kindly and peaceful man who could neither condone nor aid Black Hawk's activities in 1832. He participated in and signed the Treaty of Fort Armstrong, September 21, 1832 which ended the war. In these and future negotiations he acted as Keokuk's lieutenant and displayed his abilities as a public speaker and as a person capable of maintaining his composure. In 1837, having travelled to Washington where he, Keokuk and others signed the October 21 Treaty of Washington, Wapello delivered a number of speeches while touring several east coast cities, and underlined the Indians friendship toward the people and government of the United States.

Wapello died in present Ottumwa, Iowa, and was buried near his good friend Gen. Joseph M. Street who had accompanied his party to the east coast in 1837. A portrait of him was painted in Washington in 1837 by Charles Bird King. Wapello County, Iowa is named for him.

WARD, NANCY (Cherokee; fl. 18th century), a famous mediator between her people and whites, was a half breed Cherokee whose father was probably a British officer and whose mother was probably the sister of the chief, Attakulalculla. The dates of her birth and death are not known, but her most well-known diplomatic efforts took place between 1776 and 1781. She was known to her people as Ghigau, meaning "pretty woman" or "beloved woman." She was a member of the Cherokee war council. She owned many cattle and slaves. Ownership of property by women was a rarity among North American Indian tribes.

Nancy Ward was present at the signing of the Treaty of Hopewell on November 28, 1785, the first treaty which Cherokees made with the U.S. She spoke before the signing expressing the hopes of most Cherokees that the treaty would bring about a permanent peace between whites and Cherokees. She was consistently friendly to American settlers.

In July, 1776, the bellicose chief Dragging Canoe planned an attack on settlers living on lands whose ownership was in controversy between Cherokees and whites. Nancy Ward warned the settlers in advance of the attack, thus saving their lives. During the attack, Dragging Canoe did take two captives, one a woman whom Nancy Ward saved from death. She took the woman into her home for a short time until the woman was freed. During her captivity the white woman introduced Nancy Ward and her slaves to certain household skills such as making butter.

In 1781, the Cherokee war council chose Nancy Ward to attempt to make peace with John Sevier and his band.

WARNER, THOMAS (Carib; *c.* 1620–?), called "Carib" or "Indian" Warner, was the natural son of Sir Thomas Warner, British colonizer of the West Indies, and a Carib Indian woman from the island of Dominica. His career as an Indian leader in the Lesser Antilles was made and unmade by this possession of white and Indian blood.

Carib Warner was born about 1620, some six years after his father reached the West Indies. As a youth, he escaped from the English stronghold of St. Kitts, and soon rose to leadership among his mother's people. Warner led Carib attacks on the French settlements of Guadeloupe and Martinique, as well as against the English on St. Kitts and St. Vincent. Despite his choice of the Indian side, he was appointed in 1664 Indian governor of Dominica by Lord Francis Willoughby, Britain's administrator in the West Indies. In return Warner helped Britain take St. Lucia. In 1666 the French retook St. Lucia and captured Carib Warner. Willoughby's successor, his brother William, gained Warner's freedom in return for soon violated concessions to the French. Restored to his post, Warner was forced, in violation of the 1660 Treaty of Basse-Terre, to recognize British sovereignty in Dominica and St.

Vincent. Allegedly, Warner then began negotiating with the French.

Carib Warner's death was as controversial as his life. His English half-brother Philip landed in Dominica on Christmas day, 1674, and enlisted his aid in suppressing the rebellious Indians of the Windward Islands. Carib Warner's Leeward Indians were then set upon by the British, either in cold blood or open combat; all of the Indians were killed.

The next year, some shipwrecked black slaves landed on St. Vincent and formed with the Indians the savage tribe called the Black Caribs. The full-blooded Island Caribs thus lost in one year a strong leader and their ancient ethnic identity.

WARREN, PEARL ERNA KALLAPPA (Makah; August 13, 1911–   ), a Makah active in Seattle Indian affairs, was born in Neah Bay, Washington. Her activites include her work as executive director of the Seattle Indian Center and her efforts as a member and officer of numerous organizations involved with the issues affecting the lives of Indians.

WASHAKIE (Shoshoni; 1804—1900), "shoot (the buffalo) running," was a Shoshoni chief, of mixed Shoshoni and Umatilla blood. Before reaching maturity he left the Umatilla and joined his mother's people, the Shoshoni. Washakie was noted chiefly for his friendship toward the whites and as a warrior against his tribal enemies. He early became the chief of the Eastern Band of Shoshoni of Wyoming, known also as Washakie's Band, by reason of his prowess and leadership, but when about 70 some of the younger men aspiring to the chiefship, took steps to depose him. Washakie disappeared from the camp, and two months later, on the night when the council met to take action, he suddenly appeared with six scalps which he had taken alone on the warpath, thus setting at rest all further opposition to his chieftaincy on the ground of age.

Washakie is described as having been light in color, of commanding figure, very tall, powerfully built, and of dignified carriage, and had a reputation for great endurance. He realized the importance of his position, and was fond of form and ceremony in his dealings with white people. When in the 50s emigrants passed in large numbers through the Shoshoni country in Wyoming, Washakie and his people exercised great forbearance, following the injunctions of the Government agents to aid overland travelers in recovering strayed or lost stock, helping the emigrants across dangerous fiords, and refraining from all acts of reprisal when animals of the white men destroyed the Indian root and herding grounds. So friendly and helpful were Washakie and the members of his band that 9,000 emigrants signed a paper commending their kind treatment. Washakie owed his great popularity among his people to his exploits on the warpath, especially against the Siksika (Blackfeet) and the Crows, and also, it is asserted, because in his younger days he brooked no opposition in the tribe and allowed no asylum to a horse thief or a vagabond.

Before the battle of Bear River in 1863, in which Gen. Connor defeated the Bannock and hostile Shoshoni who refused to heed Washakie's warning, he fled with the greater portion of his tribe to Ft. Bridger, Wyoming, thus saving many of his people from destruction. When Ft. Brown was established on the site of Lander, Wyoming, in 1869, Washakie met the soldiers and avowed his friendship for the whites, and frequently served as a scout in campaigns against the Cheyenne, Sioux, Arapaho, Ute, and other hostile tribes. Members of his band also performed valiant service against the Cheyenne following the Custer defeat in 1876. At the time of his death, Feb. 20, 1900, Washakie was a devout member of the Protestant Episcopal church and a firm friend of the missionaries. He

.was buried with military honors, in the cemetery at Ft. Washakie, Wyoming, where a monument has been erected over his grave. He was succeeded by his son, known as Dick Washakie.

WATHATOTARHO (Onondaga; *c.* 1525–1590), an authentic Onondaga chief, survives in Iroquois legend as a half-monster half-human firgure who used every fiendish power at his command to obstruct the formation of the Iroquois League. With hissing snakes for hair and turtle-like hands and feet, Wathatotarho was hated and feared by all the Iroquois. When the pacifistic Hiawatha attempted to unite the five tribes into a single confederation and to stop them from practicing blood revenge on each other, Wathatotarho responded by killing Hiawatha's daughters. The evil-minded Onondaga chief comes down through legend as the antithesis and antagonist of the saintly Hiawatha.

For a while, Wathatotarho appeared victorious. Following the death of his last daughter, Hiawatha abandoned his attempts to convert the Onondagas, and he wandered off through the wilderness to other Iroquoisian tribes. The Mohawks, Oneidas, and Cayugas were more receptive to reform, but they would agree to unite only if Wathatotarho ceased his tribal tyranny and agreed to live in peace. Yet, it was not until Hiawatha joined with Dekanawida that the magic power on the side of reform and confederation could overcome Wathatotarho's dreaded sorcery on the side of evil and division.

According to Iroquois legend, Hiawatha and Dekanawida succeeded in altering Wathatotarho's ghastly appearance into that of a normal man as the first step in the conversion process. Once the Onondaga's monster-like body resembled a human being's, the two mystics converted the chief's fiendish mind to accept The Great Peace. Undoubtedly, however, there was a good deal more astute political bargaining among the three Indians than the legend takes into account. In return for his acquiescence, Wathatotarho demanded and received certain concessions that made the Onondagas the principal tribe in the newly formed League of the Five Nations. The Onondagas could send the largest number of delegates to every council session; the session itself would take place only on Onondaga territory; and the Onondaga chief—perpetually to be called "Wathatotarho"—would be the moderator and single most important member of the council. Although his name means "he obstinately refused to acquiesce," Wathatotarho's eventual agreement led to the creation of a stable government for the five Iroquois nations that was to last for two hundred years.

WATIE, STAND (Cherokee; December 12, 1806– September 7, 1871), was a Cherokee chief remembered as a brilliant Confederate soldier. Known to his people as Degata, he was born near Rome, Georgia. He was educated in a mission school. At the conclusion of his studies he returned to his home to engage in farming.

He was the brother of Elias Boudinot, founder of the first Cherokee newspaper, *Cherokee Phoenix*. He worked with Boudinot on the newspaper and became a very successful farmer prior to the Cherokee removal to Oklahoma. His status and wealth led him to combine with other wealthy Cherokees to sign the treaty of New Echota in 1835. This treaty authorized the removal of all Cherokees to Indian territory and gave the U.S. government jurisdiction over their ancestral homelands in Georgia and Tennessee. The treaty was opposed by most Cherokees and its perpertrators, with the exception of Stand Watie, were murdered in 1839.

After the removal he established himself again as a prosperous planter and became leader of the treaty party. Those who supported the New Eshota treaty represented one of three factions whose conflicts kept the new Cherokee nation in a state of turmoil until 1846.

During the Civil War, the Cherokee nation attempted to remain neutral but eventually aligned itself with the Confederacy. Stand Watie distinguished himself as a brave fighter and skillful strategist. He and his company of Cherokees fought tenanciously in the battles of Wilson's Creek and Pea Ridge. In May, 1864, the Confederate government conferred the rank of brigadier general upon him. He was one of the last Confederate officers to surrender, not doing so until June, 1865.

Upon returning to the Cherokee nation, Stand Watie led raids against those Cherokees who had supported the Union cause. He burned down the home of Chief John Ross, believing that Ross had instigated the murder of Elias Boudinot. Eventually Watie returned to his farming and business enterprises. He died on September 7, 1871.

WAUMEGESAKO (Chippewa; 1789–1844), also called The Wampum, was the head chief of a band composed of Chippewa, Potawatomi, and Ottawa. Extremely friendly to the early white settlers in Wisconsin and northern Illinois, Waumegesako played a prominent role in the treaties of Buttes des Morts (1827), Green Bay (1828), and Prairie du Chien (1829). By the terms of the treaty of Chicago, which Waumegesako signed in 1833 and which was ratified in 1835, the Indians surrendered all claim to a large tract of land in northern Illinois. In appreciation of Waumegesako's friendliness and generosity, the citizens of Manitowoc erected a monument to his memory.

WAUNEKA, ANNIE DODGE (Navajo; April 10, 1910–   ), was a Navajo woman, still active in the 1970s, who became nationally famous through her efforts to bring modern health care and education to the Navajo reservation. Her success in mixing the new culture with the old was due, at least in part, to her deep belief in the way of her people combined with the courage to propose changes she believed were better.

Annie Dodge Wauneka was born in a hogan, the traditional Navajo earth loge, on the Navajo Reservation. Her father was Henry Chee Dodge (Kiilchii); her mother was K'eehabah. Henry Dodge was a self-made man—a wealthy rancher and a respected leader in the Navajo tribe. Separated from his family during fighting between federal troops and Navajo in the 1860s, he learned to speak English while a child at Fort Sumner, and later became an interpreter for the government at Fort Defiance. His wife K'eehabah was with him for less than two years. She became his wife, as per Navajo custom, while his other two wives, distant cousins of K'eehabah, were tending their herds elsewhere. When they returned, Annie was raised in her father's home with her half-brothers Tom and Ben and her half-sister Mary. She had lived away from her father, in her mother's hogan, for about a year.

Annie's upbringing was a fabric woven from traditional elements of Navajo culture and white culture. Thus, although she did many things unusual for a Navajo girl, things that put her in close contact with the increasingly important white culture, she also was instilled with a strong set of traditional Navajo values. In her later life, she said, "An Indian is an Indian. Her belief is within her. Her heritage is within her. She may have a dark complexion. She may have a light complexion. She may have blue eyes. She may not have. But she is an Indian." (Steiner, *New Indians*, p. 225). Like other Navajo girls her age, Annie was trusted as the family sheepherder when she was no older than five. She was given lambs each year by her father, which would become the nucleus of her own flock when she married, and each year even when she was away in school, she spent spring at home to help with the lambing. She also grew up in the traditional Navajo religion.

Her environment and some of her activities were unusual, however. Although born in a traditional hogan—her mother's—she was raised in her father's home, an un-Navajo-like ranch house with a porch, that had been designed by an architect from Flagstaff, Arizona. The home was comfortably furnished, and had a library. Annie's father also fenced his land, contrary to Navajo custom. In addition, during a period when most Navajo distrusted whites and would hold curative ceremonies for tribal members who had come into extensive contact with white culture, the elder Dodge sent all his children to boarding schools. Annie Dodge went to the government school at Fort Defiance, Arizona, beginning classes on her 8th birthday and attending through the fifth grade. Then she transferred to the Albuquerque Indian School in New Mexico, where she was moved ahead rapidly and had completed 11th grade by the time she quit school at 18 years old. Several events occurred while Annie was in school that shaped the course of her future life. While in the school in Albuquerque, she met another Navajo student, George Wauneka, who was to become her future husband. During that period also, her father was named chairman of the Navajo Tribal Council, and with several other tribal leaders, visited Annie's school. He spoke on the importance of education while there, and his ideas formed an important part of his daughter's philosophy in later life. While at the Fort Defiance school, Annie had been exposed to two epidemics, flu and trachoma. The flu epidemic left many children dead, and while quarantined at the school, Annie helped the school nurse, and was deeply moved by the need for proper health care among her people. This realization also was to shape her future life.

Besides her schooling, there were other occurrences in Annie Wauneka's childhood that made her different from other Navajo girls. One biographer notes that, unlike her sister Mary, the younger Dodge girl was not given a puberty ceremony, the traditional Navajo rite that indicates a girl is ready for marriage, upon her return from school. Neither did she attend a number of squaw dances, important social events for young Navajo men and women. It is reported that at the first and only dance to which her parents brought her, at the age of 13, she was so embarrassed over what she felt was a lack of social skills and ability to dance that she hid under the seat of her parents wagon the whole night.

Upon her return from school at 18, Mrs. Wauneka took up sheepherding for the family again. One biography suggests that Mrs. Wauneka was not treated equally with the other three children and that, in fact, there may have been some friction between them. But this split, if it existed, must have been at least in part assuaged by the amount of time Annie Wauneka began to spend with her father, by the interest he took in her and the responsibility he gave her. He had been chairman of the Navajo Business Council until 1928, the year his youngest daughter returned from school, and after that continued to take a leading role in the government of the Navajo tribe. He supported the stock reduction program proposed by the federal government in the 1930s and worked diligently to explain it to the tribe.

Their acceptance of it constituted a major change in Navajo custom. Throughout this period, both before Annie Wauneka's marriage to George Wauneka in October 1929 and after, Dodge took his daughter with him to meetings, helped her hone her interpretive skills to a delicate edge, and encouraged her to understand the issues involved and the politicking behind the decisions and to speak her mind. He was, as he had when he sent her to school, encouraging her to take a non-traditional path, for Navajo custom was that only men should take leadership in the councils. In later years, Mrs. Wauneka described her philosophy about women in government this way: "We are all human beings. To me it doesn't really matter whether it's a woman, or whether it's a man. Their structure is the same. They have a brain to think with. This is what I always base my opinion on in dealing with people.

To my way of thinking there should be woman leadership as there should be man. Because the problem remains. And the problem affects both sex. If a leader is needed, although it is a woman, I would say it should be used." (Steiner, *New Indians*, pp. 225 and 226.)

After her marriage, Mrs. Wauneka went to live with her new husband on her father's property near Window Rock, Arizona, where they herded not only Dodge's sheep and cattle, but their own as well. There, at Klagetoh, the Waunekas raised six children: Georgia Ann, born in 1931, Henry in 1933, Irma in 1935, Franklin in 1945, Lorencita in 1947, and Sallie in 1950. Two of Annie Wauneka's children, born between 1935 and 1945, died. In the 1970s, the Wauneka's still ranched out of Klagetoh.

Annie Wauneka continued to accompany her father to meetings as well as working with her husband on the ranch. During the 1930s and 1940s, she worked with him to bring day schools, a water development program, an environmental conservation program, and a Civil Conservation Corps to the reservation. It is reported that Dodge once told her "Do not let my straight rope fall to the ground. If you discover it dropping, quickly pick it up and hold it aloft." Upon her father's death in 1947, this is what Annie Wauneka did.

She began by working for the chapter of the tribal council in Klagetoh, Arizona, as secretary and interpreter. As part of her job, she visited hospitals and interpreted for the Navajo there who could not speak English. Four years later, in 1951, the reputation of her work had become so strong that she was elected a delegate to the Navajo Tribal Council from the Klagetoh district. The election was a high honor, for the Navajo had never before elected a woman to their tribal council. Mrs. Wauneka continued to be elected every four years, even when challenged for her seat by men, and in the 1970s, she was still serving on the council.

Her primary concern was Indian health. A big killer on the reservation was tuberculosis. The Navajo were unfamiliar with and distrustful of Western theories of disease, but the traditional Navajo curing practices upon which they relied— chanting ceremonies performed by medicine men—proved largely ineffective against tuberculosis. Even those who were persuaded to seek treatment in Western hospitals frequently ran away, back to their homes, contributing to the spread of the disease. Soon after her election, Mrs. Wauneka was chosen chairperson of the Health and Welfare Committee, and she waded full-scale into the problem of irradicating the disease. First she spent three months learning from U.S. Public Health Service personnel as much as she could about the Western concept of the disease. Then she took this information back to the reservation, and by working closely with Navajo medicine men and patients, helped mobilize a cooperative effort between Western and Indian medicine that was highly successful. Her efforts included visiting with patients in the hospitals to bring them news from home, finding runaways and explaining to them the dangers of coming home before being cured, and writing a dual language glossary to help white and red medicine men understand each other. In it, "germs" became "bugs that eat the body," the closest Navajo equivalent.

When tuberculosis control was well under way, Mrs. Wauneka began other projects. She urged her tribespeople to use the new clinics being built on the reservation, and through educational movies and her own radio program broadcast in Navajo from Gallup, New Mexico, explained the principles of sanitation and health care. She toured the reservation to get support for a proposal, later accepted in part by the tribal council, that money be provided to put glass windows and wooden floors in dirt-floored hogans to allow for more healthful living conditions. She also helped her people learn about the dangers of gastroenteritis and alcoholism.

A second major concern of Mrs. Wauneka was education. She believed her father's words, that in education was the salvation of Navajos in competition with white culture, and in her years on the tribal council was a persistent proponent of educational programs such as scholarships, tribal control of schools and improved roads to make schools more accessible. During her membership on the council, the tribe established a $10 million scholarship trust fund, and many schools were built on the reservation, including the Navajo Community College in Many Farms, Arizona. Since belief in the Navajo culture including language, religion, and dress, had always been a strong part of her life, and she was also well aware of the dangers of sending children away to be educated as well as the important contributions to wage-earning and self-esteem that education could make, Mrs. Wauneka formulated her educational philosophy this way: "Indian parents must have a say in where schools are to be located," she advises. "Children should be allowed to remain closer to their homes, and their parents should have a close connection with their schools." "We are a half-century behind the rest of the country. We want to keep our children near us, not send them miles away to a school where we cannot supervise them, but until we can, we must accept the education that we have, for it is the answer to our problems." (Gridley, *Contemporary American Indian Leaders*, pp 193 to 194.)

By the 1970s, Mrs. Wauneka's activities and recognition of them extended well beyond the Navajo reservation. She had served on New Mexico's Committee in the Aging and had attended conferences in Alaska and Washington, D.C., as a member of advisory boards to the U.S. Surgeon General and the U.S. Public Health service. She had received numerous awards, including the Indian

Achievement Award of the Indian Council Fire in 1959 and, in December, 1964, the Presidential Medal of Freedom, the nation's highest civilian honor. Pope John XXIII and Pres. John F. Kennedy received Medals of Freedom at the same ceremony.

In 1974, Annie Dodge Wauneka was re-elected to the Navajo Tribal Council. She continued to work with the Indian people, the Indian government and the white government, the young and the old, and continued to balance within herself the unique blend of tradition and change through which she had been able to do so much good for her people.

WEATHERFORD, WILLIAM (Creek; *c.* 1780–March 9, 1824), also Red Cloud was a cruel and dissolute Creek chief who mended his ways following the massacre of Creek warriors at Horseshoe Bend (1813). It is not known exactly who William Weatherford's parents were. His mother may have been a full-blooded Seminole, or she may have been a half-sister to the great Creek chieftain of the 18th century: Alexander McGillivray. Weatherford's father may have been the wealthy Scottish (or English) merchant Charles Weatherford, or he may have been an itinerant peddler. In any case, William Weatherford developed into a tall and well-proportioned warrior and possessed a special gift for oratory.

Nevertheless, most whites on the frontier at that time hated him, accusing the Creek chief of the basest violations of personal morality. Although Tecumseh urged Weatherford to go to war as early as 1811, he delayed until 1813, by which time his cause was already lost. In that year, he led his followers into the Creek War. On August 30, 1813, 1,000 Creek warriors massacred 500 whites at Fort Mims. The victims, including women and children, suffered cruelly before they were put to death. It was all of this, naturally, that won Weatherford the detestation of frontier whites.

In 1814, the Creek War concluded with the Battle of Horseshe Bend. The Creeks under Weatherford and Menewa had been driven back by the forces of General Andrew Jackson, until finally Weatherford decided to take a stand at the great bend of the Tallapoosa River. Jackson utterly destroyed the 1,000 Creeks at Horseshoe Bend, thereby ending the war. Weatherford surrendered himself to Jackson, who then released the chief upon receiving Weatherford's assurance that the Creeks would remain at peace.

William Weatherford's last years witnessed a definite improvement in his behavior; he took on a greater degree of dignity as he lived more soberly and industriously. The chief lived on a fairly prosperous plantation among white people in Monroe County, Alabama. He married a white woman (his third wife) in 1817, and his many children also intermarried with whites. Weatherford died on March 9, 1824—saved from having to see his people removed from their homes to the west. The chief was buried in the land of his ancestors.

WELCH, EARL (Chickasaw; January 27, 1892–November 12, 1969), a Chickasaw Indian, served as a justice on the Supreme Court of the state of Oklahoma from 1932–65 and was Chief Justice from 1941–43 and 1957–59. He was born near Wister in Indian Territory (now Oklahoma). His judicial career marred by charges of bribery and corruption, he resigned from the bench in March, 1965 to avoid impeachment. He died in Oklahoma.

WENDJIMADUB (Chippewa; *c.* 1838– *c.* 1910), distinguished himself as a courageous chief when, in 1878, he defended a white agent opposed by several chiefs in council. A veteran of the Civil War (he served with a Minnesota regiment), Wendjimadub made his living as a farmer, although he was sufficiently wealthy that he seldom had to perform any labor himself. The Chippewa chief—head of a band of about 40—was already a noted orator prior to his vigorous defense of agent Louis Stowe. Stowe had proved himself an honest and competent agent, but a half-breed trader wanted Stowe replaced by someone who would further the trader's own illicit schemes, and he convinced the other chiefs to demand that Stowe be fired. In a council before several prominent government officials, therefore, Wendjimadub stood alone in proclaiming Stowe's innocence of the charges leveled by the chiefs.

WETAMOO (Pocasset; *c.* 1635– August 6, 1676), called the Squaw Sachem of the Pocasset, allied her people with Philip, chief of the Wampanoags, during King Philip's War of 1675– 76. Wetamoo was the widow of Philip's brother Alexander, and her husband's death following close upon a severe interrogation by the Plymouth colonial authorities had a great deal to do with the animosity both she and Philip felt toward the English settlers. When Philip led his braves on the warpath, Westamoo joined him, bringing not only her own Pocasset tribe but also a substantial band of Narragansets under her second husband, Quinnapin.

On August 6, 1676, one of Philip's warriors turned traitor and led the colonists to Wetamoo's camp. She escaped, but then drowned in the Taunton River during her flight. When they found her body, the colonists cut off Wetamoo's head and mounted it on a pole in Plymouth to serve as an example to any other potentially hostile natives.

WHIRLWIND (Cayuse).

WHITE ANTELOPE (Cheyenne).

WHITE BUFFALO (Cheyenne) was a chief in the early 1900s.

WHITE CALF (Piegan) was the last Piegan chief, probably in the 1890s. He died in 1903.

WHITE EYES (Delaware; ?– November 1778), because of his light-colored eyes, the Delaware war captain Koquethagecthan, also spelled Coquetakeghton ("that which is put near the head") was called White Eyes, sometimes Grey Eyes. Possibly there was white ancestry in his background. The date and place of his birth are unknown, but in 1762 he was living at a Delaware Indian town at the mouth of Beaver Creek, a tributary of the Ohio, south of Pittsburgh. With other migrant Delawares, whose original homes were in the Delaware River area, he moved to the Muskingum valley in Tuscarawas County, Ohio prior to the American Revolution.

Colonel George Morgan, Indian agent for the Continental Congress, became a good friend of White Eyes, and persuaded him to use his influence to consolidate the Delawares at a new location at present Coshocton, Ohio. There a new council fire was kindled.

Small in stature, but resolute, brave, and highly intelligent, White Eyes was selected in 1776 by the Delaware Great Council to replace the aging and infirm principal chief, Netawatwees. He appeared before the Congress in Philadelphia where he was officially thanked for promoting peace between the Delawares and the whites. Congress gave him $300 and two fine horses with saddles and bridles.

White Eyes agreed that in the event of war with the British, the Delawares would aid the Americans, and he proposed that the Delaware tribe should constitute a fourteenth state in the American union. These points were incorporated in a treaty at Pittsburgh, September 17, 1778, of which he, John Killbuck, Jr., and Captain Pipe were signatories.

He was commissioned a lieutenant-colonel, and while serving as a guide for troops under command of General Lachlan McIntosh, was murdered in November 1778 by an unknown assailant. Following his death a pro-British faction seized control of

the tribe and persuaded the majority of the Delaware warriors to raise their tomahawks against the
Americans. This hostility broke the treaty of 1778,
and alienated Americans from the Delawares.

George White Eyes and Joseph White Eyes were
two of the chief's sons, but the names of his wife and
other children are not known.

WHITE HAIR (Osage; ?–August, 1825), properly
known as Pawhuska or Pahuska and also known as
Teshuhimga and Cahagatonga, was the early 19th
century chief of the Great or Big Osage whose village was in the southwestern part of Missouri in
present Vernon County. White Hair was a usurper.
He and the tribe's nominal chief, Cashesegra, were
established in their posts by the trader Pierrre
Chouteau for his own economic gain. Although the
lawful chief, Claremont (Claremore), was very
young when White Hair took over, he later became
an influential warrior who led a faction within the
tribe opposed to White Hair. At times Claremont
acted in spite of and in place of White Hair especially in dealing with the Cherokee. Because White
Hair had usurped his post, many of his warriors felt
they owed him no allegiance whatsoever. They
joined the Arkansas Osage.

In 1806 Zebulon Pike established his Camp Independence near White Hair's village. When Pike directed White Hair to come to his camp, instead of
mustering the dignity his people expected and
demanding Pike to attend him, White Hair immediately went to Camp Independence. He was unable
to control his warriors. When Pike requested scouts,
horses, supplies for his expeditions, White Hair had
so little influence that he was barely able to supply
anything at all. When an action or stand appeared
unpopular among his people, White Hair was un-
willing to do anything. Although he opposed it, he
could not stop a continuation of hostilities against
the Arkansas white settlers.

White Hair signed a number of treaties with the

U.S. government including a treaty at St. Louis on September 25, 1818 readjusting the Osage northern boundaries and ceding land to the U.S., and the June 2, 1825 treaty under which the Osage removed to Kansas. White Hair died at his village shortly after August, 1825.

WHITEHORSE, HARRY (Sauk-Winnebago; 1928–), works with metal, sometimes as a mechanic and repairer of automobile bodies and sometimes as a sculptor. A Sauk-Winnebago, born in 1928, his workshop in Madison, Wisconsin, is filled with scrap metal that he pounds into sculptures with a stylized realism that reflect his attention to anatomical detail. His statues and occasional paintings also portray his regard for nature. Exhibitions of his work include the 1968 Olympic Committee, the Alcoa Aluminum Company, and the Credit Union National Association.

WHITE MAN RUNS HIM (Crow) or Marschecoodo, born in 1854, was one of Custer's scouts.

WHITE-NOSED FOX (Sauk).

WHITE PIGEON (Potawatomi; fl. 19th century), a chief of the Potawatomi, saved a white community from an Indian massacre. White Pigeon, while in the area of Detroit around the year 1812, learned of an impending Indian uprising. He went to the town which was to be attacked (now White Pigeon, Michigan) and warned the settlers—a warning which undoubtedly saved their lives. The Potawatomi chief is also noted for his signing the Greenville Treaty (August 3, 1795) and the Treaty of Brownstown (November 25, 1808). He died about the age of 30 and was buried on the outskirts of the town in St. Joseph County, Michigan that now bears his name. A monument was erected to his memory in 1909.

WHITE SWAN (Yakima) was chief of the Yakima in 1900.

WILD CAT (Seminole) or *Coacoochee* was the son of King Philip (Ematla).

WILD HOG (Cheyenne; fl. 19th century), a principal chief of the northern Cheyenne, prominent in the 1878–79 uprising, when, with Dull Knife and Little Wolf, he led his people from Indian Territory, in present Oklahoma, to the Sand Hills in Nebraska. There they surrendered on October 23, 1878 to troops under Captain J. B. Johnson and were taken to Camp Robinson. When the Indians refused to return to Indian Territory, commanding officers tried to starve them into submission. Wild Hog was put in irons until most of his people had been killed or captured, then taken to Dodge City, Kansas, a few months later.

WILLIAM I (Mosquito; ?–1879), William Henry Clarence, was the last Mosquito Indian king to enjoy even limited powers on Nicaragua's British-controlled Mosquito Coast. Successor in 1865 of George V, William I was the father of the last Mosquito king, Robert II. William died in 1879, and was succeeded by his uncle, George VI.

WILLOYA, EMMA (Inuit; July 15, 1898–   ), represents the needs of her Eskimo people on numerous boards. She was born at Fort Barrow, Alaska. Her work as an agent for the Office of Price Administration in Nome received recognition by Presidents Roosevelt and Truman. She has served as manager of the Nome Skin Sewers Association and devotes her efforts to helping women make and sell their handmade products.

WILSON, ALFRED (Cheyenne; 1878–February, 1945), a devoted leader of the Native American Church (NAC), pledged himself and his followers to the struggle of winning recognition and freedom from persecution for his religious beliefs. A Southern Cheyenne, he was born in 1878. The peyote *cult* from this period was eventually incorporated into the NAC in Oklahoma in 1918. The religion combines elements from pre-Columbian and Christian beliefs into its ceremonies. From the beginning, however, it was a controversial faith because of the use of peyote in the worship rituals. Wilson offered to submit himself to unlimited scientific investifation to disprove the charges the peyote was a dangerous drug. In 1940 the Navajo Tribal Council outlawed the use of peyote on the reservations. The NAC was already on the defensive and by 1944 had moved to incorporate as a national organization. Wilson was chosen as a delegate at large from Normal, Oklahoma in that year. He died in February, 1945. It was not until the 1960s that the laws began turning in favor of the NAC, and the Supreme Court defended the NAC as a legitimate church entitled to First Amendment protection.

WILSON, DR. JAMES J. III (Dakota; 20th century), an educator and administrator, is a Dakota-Oglala Sioux who was born on the Pine Ridge Reservation in South Dakota. He received his Ed.D. from Arizona State University, taught education and psychology, and served as chief of the Indian Division of the Office of Economic Opportunity. After leaving the OEO in 1969, he became head of the Southwestern Cooperative Educational Laboratory in Albuquerque, New Mexico.

WINAMAC (Potawatomi; fl. 19th century), a principal chief of the Potawatomi, fought with the British during the War of 1812. Winamac earned the wrath of Tecumseh in 1809 when he signed a treaty which ceded a great deal of Potawatomi land in central Indiana to the United States; Tecumseh even threatened to kill the Potawatomi chief. Winamac, though swung over to the Shawnee chief's side, lead his warriors against Harrison's forces at Tippecanoe and later joining the British during the War of 1812. For his hostility to the Americans, Winamac lost his life; he was killed on November 22, 1812 by a pro-U.S. Shawnee chief named Captain James Logan.

WINNEMUCCA, SARAH (Paiute; *c.* 1844–October 16, 1891), was an Indian peacemaker unafraid to champion the cause of peace with the whites among her own Northern Paiute tribe, even when it was unpopular, and just as unafraid to expose the corruption of the white officials who were taking advantage of her people. She was one of the first Indians in Nevada to receive white education and in turn helped promote it among her people.

Sarah Winnemucca, whose Indian name apparently was Jocmeton, was born about 1844. She was a Northern Paiute and was probably born near Humboldt Lake in western Nevada. Winnemucca's band, of which she was a part, was seminomadic, roving from Honey Lake in northeastern California to the region of Pyramid Lake, Carson Sink, and Humboldt Sink in western Nevada. At the time of her birth, white emigrants were just beginning to come in contact with the Northern Paiute. Records show that the Chiles party of settlers passed through Northern Paiute country in 1842, the Chiles-Walker party in 1843, and the Stevens-Murphy party in 1844. Before this time, Northern Paiute had probably only met occasional white trappers. Contact with the white emigrants, who brought a new culture as well as mystifying but exciting implements such as guns and tin plates, profoundly affected Sarah's grandfather, Winnemucca, who was an important Paiute chief. It is not known whether Sarah believed, as her grandfather did, in the mythical family in which the white men and red men were children of the same parents, but from her later life, it is obvious Sarah was deeply affected by her grandfather's heartfelt desire to welcome the whites as family and work through without anger the differences bound to arise when two widely different cultures met.

Much of what is known about Sarah's childhood comes from her own accounts, which are highly detailed but in some cases apparently are chronologically inaccurate. Her grandfather, Chief Winnemucca, guided white emigrants and explorers who ventured through Northern Paiute country, and he apparently accompanied the expedition of Capt. John C. Frémont to California in 1845 with 11 other Northern Paiute. He was named "Capt. Truckee" by Frémont or members of an earlier expedition. It is unclear from Sarah's accounts how many times her grandfather went to California, and whether the events following his first trip which she described from memory or later reconstructions, affected her childhood, but before his death in about 1859, the elder Winnemucca went to California at least twice. His first trip was as a guide with Frémont, and his second and possibly third were as leader of parties of emigrants from the Northern Paiute nation. He was convinced that the way of the future lay in the California country, rich in natural resources, and in friendship with the whites, who possessed such amazing tools. Sarah vividly described how, upon or or another of her grandfather's returns from California, he sat and talked to his people for days about the kindness of the whites, their houses, ships, and cannon. He had brought with him guns, uniforms with brass buttons, and apparently samples of writing, perhaps telegrams, to justify his enthusiasm. When he began leading migrations west, he appointed Sarah's father chief. On one of his trips, Sarah, her mother, and her brother Natchez accompanied him to California, but it is unclear how long Sarah stayed there.

From Sarah's accounts, meetings between the whites and her tribespeople during her childhood were not always friendly. During one of her grandfather's absences, the word spread through hers and neighboring tribes that emigrating whites were killing Indians without reason, and guided by Sarah's father, the Northern Paiute stored food for the winter and then hid in the mountains. But a party of whites, possibly the Donner party, discovered the food and inexplicably burned it. The next year, Sarah's father called the tribe together in a 5 day feast to warn them about a dream he had had, showing a great migration of whites in which many Indians were senselessly killed. When Sarah's grandfather returned from California, however, he still counciled peace with the whites, and maintained his position even after Sarah's uncle and several other Northern Paiutes were killed by whites while on a fishing trip to the Humboldt River. Again, her grandfather's desire to maintain peace with the whites despite friction made a deep impression on Sarah, for she describes the scene in which he called the tribe together to council peace, with his own son one of the dead, in great detail.

Sarah's grandfather died in about 1859. As one of his last requests, he asked that Sarah and her sister Mary be sent to the Sisters' School in San Jose, California. Sarah made the trip in 1860 and attended school for a short time, perhaps as little as three weeks. But from this instruction and perhaps other which she may have received from white families such as the Ormsley family in Carson Valley, Nevada, with whom she and her sister lived in about 1860, for example, she learned to read and write English. The Winnemucca sisters were two of a few, and perhaps the only, Indians in Nevada with any formal schooling before 1865.

It was while Sarah was staying at the Ormsley's (or Ormsbey's) that she was exposed to another incident which shaped her life. According to Sarah's account three Washoe Indian men were turned over to white authorities who executed them for the murder of two whites. The Indians apparently were not given a trial, but were shot while trying to escape. Sarah further states that several months later the white authorities decided that two whites had committed the murders, and hung them. It may be seen that in her childhood, Sarah was motivated to be friends with the whites by her grandfather and was also shown, by incidents such as the one in 1860, that her people would have to work to maintain their rights. As an adult, she worked to accomplish these two tasks.

Beginning in the 1860s, relations between the Northern Paiute and the whites, which, before had been fairly peaceful, began to be marred by friction. Occasionally, hostility broke out between the Northern Paiute and miners and emigrants. The Bannock Indians to the north of the Northern Paiute were involved even more frequently in incidents with the whites. The whites reacted by confining the Northern Paiute first on a reservation around Pyramid Lake in 1864, and then in 1875, removing them to the Walker Reservation in eastern Oregon, where they were settled with the Bannock. Confinement on a reservation did not please the Indians, and they had increasing trouble with unscrupulous whites who administered the reservations. In 1866, Sarah, who had been living in Virginia City, came to live on the reservation with her brother, following the deaths of her mother and sister. In 1868, Sarah, who could speak English well, became an interpreter for the Indian agent, F. Dodge, helping him in dealing with the Shoshoni. She may also have interpreted for agent C. A. Batemen, agent to her own tribe. Apparently she also managed to get interviews with James W. Nye, then governor of Nevada, and with army officers who influenced Indian policy, and from them won promises of more food and clothing for her people. The 1860s saw her become increasingly dissatisfied with the treatment of the Indians by the whites, however. Settlers took some of their best land, often drove off their game and left them destitute in the winters, and the Indian agents, by her accounts, had no sympathy for their charges and were only interested in getting rich. Sarah began to agitate for improved treatment of the Indians in about 1870. She wrote letters to Major Henry Douglas, Superintendent of Indian Affairs for Nevada, to Ely S. Parker, Commissioner of Indian Affairs, and in July, 1871, visited Brigadier General E. O. C. Ord in San Francisco by request of her tribe to protest conditions. In part, she told the general "We have asked the Agents of the different reservations to help us, but all to no avail, only to be put off with another promise, so that many of the Indians of the Pyramid reservation having become dissatisfied and being on the borders of starvation, have left their houses and wandered we know not where. But they say they will not work for these Agents, for by so doing they enrich these Agents and come to absolute poverty and degradation themselves, and we would all much rather be slain and put out of our misery than to be lingering here — each day bringing new sorrows — and finally die of hunger and starvation.

We know full well that the Government has been, and is still willing to provide us with all we need, but I must inform you that it never gets past these Agents hands, but they reap all the benefit while we have all the suffering." [*Nevada Indians Speak*, 99–100]. She was supported in her claim by Major General J. M. Schofield. After her return to the reservation, although the army was more amenable to Indian requests, the agents, under orders from the Indian Bureau, tried to obstruct the efforts of Sarah and had her brother jailed for a short time. About this time, Sarah married a Lieutenant Barlett, who was stationed at Camp McDermit, Nevada. But when he was transferred back east before 1875, he divorced her and left her behind in Nevada.

In 1875, Sarah moved with her father to the Walker Reservation, and for a short time operated an Indian school there. Conditions on the reservation deteriorated, however, and there was increasing friction between the Bannock Indians and neighboring whites. When it looked as if her father would no longer be able to keep his braves peaceful and they would join the Bannock, Sarah left for Washington, D.C., in hopes of winning concessions for her tribe. But having got no further than Idaho, she was called back by news that many young Northern Paiute braves had joined the Bannock and taken her father and his supporters to the Bannock camp against their will. She was able to get the army forces under Gen. O. O. Howard to postpone their attack on the Bannock and somehow managed to enter the Bannock camp secretly and obtain the release of her father and his band. During the remainder of the Bannock War of 1877– 78, she served as Gen. O. O. Howard's interpreter.

Although Sarah helped Howard, her assistance in no way indicated she had stopped distrusting Indian agents or given up her efforts to correct conditions on the Walker Reservation. Added to her old grievances was a new one: some Northern Paiute captured in the Bannock War had been confined on the Yakima Reservation in Washington, and although now peaceful, were not being allowed to return to their own tribe. Sarah travelled to Vancouver, Washington, in 1879 where she told General Howard of her peoples' problems, and then went to San Francisco and lectured about the Paiute plight. On her way east with her brother Natchez, her lecture tour was interrupted by a telegram from Special Agent J. M. Haworth of the Office of Indian Affairs. Haworth had been ordered by his superiors in Washington, D.C., to bring the Winnemucccas there for negotiations, perhaps to halt damaging publicity engendered by their lecture tour. Sarah accepted the invitation, but persuaded the agent to stop in Winnemucca, Nevada, to confer with her people before she, her brother, her father Chief Winnemucca, and another Northern Paiute delegate journeyed to Washington with Haworth in January, 1880. There they expressed dissatisfaction over the situation on the Walker Reservation and over the fate of their people on the Yakima Reservation. They met Pres. Rutherford B. Hayes briefly, and were promised by government officials they would be given more supplies upon their return and that the Yakima prisoners would be released. Neither of these conditions were later fulfilled, although while in the capital, Sarah desisted from lecturing as the request of Haworth.

The Winnemucca delegation returned to Oregon, and Sarah was made official interpreter on the Walker Reservation early in 1880. In 1881 she opened an Indian school at Vancouver Barracks, Washington, but it lasted only a short time. In 1881 or 1882, Sarah married a Lieutenant Hopkins. Also in 1881–82, she visited her old home on the Pyramid Lake Reservation and then went east a second time, this time lecturing about the Indian situation. To further explain the situation, she wrote a book, *Life Among the Paiutes, Their Wrongs and Claims* (1882 or 1883). Then she returned to Nevada, settled on a ranch near Lovelock with her husband, and again opened an Indian school.

Sarah ran the school for three or four years, but local whites, spurred apparently by Indian agents who she had exposed, attacked her reputation. Gen. Howard and other officials defended her, but when her husband became ill with tuberculosis, the pressures became too great, and she closed the school. Her husband died about 1886, and after working as a maid for a white family to earn travelling expenses, she went to live with her sister in Morida, Montana, where she died on Oct. 16, 1891. There are indications in literature about Sarah that her closing days were unhappy, perhaps caused by loneliness, but the hints are unexplained.

WITT, SHIRLEY (Mohawk; 20th century), a physical anthropologist, was a member of the National Indian Youth Council (founded 1961) during its formative years. A Mohawk, she is currently a professor of anthropology at Colorado College, Colorado Springs, having received her Ph.D. in anthropology from the University of New Mexico in 1969.

WOLF CHIEF (Cheyenne) was also called *Honniiwigoi.*

WOLF PLUME (Blackfoot).

WOODENLEGS, JOHN, (Cheyenne; 20th century), in his early years, lived with his grandfather Richard Woodenlegs and grandmother, Daisy. This woman walked back to Montana from Oklahoma in 1878. Richard fought in the Custer battle.

He attended schools in Lame Deer, government school in Lapwai, Idaho; Busby school in Montana and Flandreau in South Dakota.

He has worked as a cowboy, coal miner, road worker, and rancher. He was manager of a Tribal Steer Herd about 4 years; was on the Tribal Council numerous terms; served as vice-president several terms, then became president in 1955 and served until September 1968. During his terms as president, the economic and social condition of the Northern Cheyennes underwent much change and improvement.

President Johnson appointed him as the only Indian member of his 25 member National Advisory Commission on Rural Poverty. This commission made a comprehensive study of rural life in America and made its report and recommendations for action in 1967.

In 1967, Woodenlegs was appointed by then Commissioner of Indian Affairs, Robert Bennett to serve on the National Indian Education Advisory Committee. This group functions in an advisory capacity on education to the Bureau of Indian Affairs Washington office.

Woodenlegs also served on an advisory committee for a national study of American Indian Education, headed by Robert Havighurst of the University of Chicago. The report of this study was issued in December 1970.

Woodenlegs has been president of the Northern Cheyenne Native American Church since about 1948. He is also a delegate-at-large of the national church organization.

Since 1968 Woodenlegs has been working full time in Indian education as a fieldworker of the Association on American Indian Affairs. He serves on advisory committees of the Bilingual Education Program, Upward Bound and Career Opportunities Program. He was a part time counselor to students at the University of Montana in a special program called the "Graduate Program in American Indian Arts". He teaches classes on Cheyenne history and culture at elementary, high school and college level, as well as speaking by invitation before groups of all kinds. He participates in many educational conferences and workshops. He is chairman of both the Northern Cheyenne Research and Human Development Association, Inc. and its Education Planning Committee. The work being done by the Association involves collection of information from elders, research into historical materials and artifacts, development of new curricula on Cheyenne history and culture for both elementary levels and adult level, and development of classroom materials for use in this curricula. The Planning Committee also sponsors an annual workshop for all reservation teachers to help educate them about Cheyenne history and culture.

WOODRING, CARL (Osage; Dec. 6, 1920—   ), an Osage painter and sculptor, was born in Kansas City, Kansas. His career includes eleven years of service with the United States Air Force and work as an architectural engineer. His paintings have achieved international recognition and have been exhibited, for example, at the Brussel's World Fair. In 1959 he published *Oklahoma Today*.

WOVOKA (Paiute; 1856–?) mystical prophet and magician, counseled the defeated tribes of the West to perform the Ghost Dance which would miraculously restore primitive life as it had been before the coming of the whites. Raised in the home of a devoutly religious white family, Wovoka was commonly known as Jack Wilson among non-Indians. When in late 1888 he suffered from a dangerous fever, Wovoka became delirious and claimed to receive revelations from the Great Spirit. The humble Paiute prophesied that the Indians' messiah was coming, an event which required a special dance to be performed. Then, the messiah would cause all the settlers, soldiers, and government agents to vanish; the plains would once again be filled with buffalo; and the living and the dead Indian brethren would be reunited.

The various tribes on reservations between the Missouri River and the Rocky Mountains sent pilgrims to Wovoka, who taught them his messaniac vision based on the Ghost Dance. To natives whose spirits had been broken through military conquest and liquor, the Paiute's prophecy meant the salvation of everything for which they longed. Soon, nearly all the tribes of the interior basin were performing the Ghost Dance and singing songs about a future filled with buffalo but no white men.

Although there was nothing in Wovoka's message or dance that called for overt resistance to white rule, the Ghost Dance did lead in precisely such a direction. When the Sioux of the Standing Rock Agency in the Dakotas began to chant and dance, the authorities there began to worry. When—fearing an uprising—the government agents attempted to arrest Sitting Bull, the aged medicine man resisted and was killed. His death was all the spark that the precarious situation needed to explode. Sioux men, women, and children ran off the reservation, but they were hunted down and massacred at Wounded Knee, South Dakota on December 29, 1890. That tragic event represented the last major Indian resistance in North America, and it was not long before Wovoka's dance and doctrine had largely disappeared.

WRIGHT, ALLEN (Chocktaw; 1825–?), was a Choctaw preacher remembered for his religious and political work on behalf of his people. Born in 1825 in Mississippi he emigrated to Indian territory with his parents in 1832. Enroute they died, leaving him and his sister orphans. For a time during his youth he lived with the family of Rev. Cyrus Kingsbury. It was under the tutelage of this prominent minister, long a friend to Indians, that Wright converted to Christianity and began to study for the ministry.

He began his studies at the Spencer Academy in the Choctaw nation. Eventually he studied at Union College in Schenectady, New York, and was graduated in 1852. After graduation, he went to New York to study at Union Theological Seminary. He was graduated in 1855 and ordained one year later. Upon returning to Indian territory, Wright established himself as a preacher and a translator. In 1873 he translated the Chickasaw constitution into Choctaw. In 1880 he published a Choctaw dictionary and shortly before his death he translated certain Hebrew psalms into Choctaw.

The Choctaw held Wright in such high regard that they elected him to political office several times. He was a member of both the House of Representatives and Senate of the Choctaw nation and later its treasurer. In 1866 Wright was sent to Washington to negotiate a new treaty for the Choctaws with the U.S. The Civil War had caused many new problems for the Choctaws, especially the status and citizenship of freedmen on Choctaw lands. While in Washington Wright was elected chief of the Choctaw nation. He held the post until 1870.

He was loved by his people and highly respected by whites who had contact with him. He married soon after graduation from Union Theological Seminary. Several of his children became prominent in Choctaw affairs as adults.

WRIGHT, JULES (Athabascan; 1933–), served as president of the Fairbanks Native Association. An Athabascan, he was born in Nenana, Alaska. Professionally he is a contractor, but from 1967– 69 he was a Republican representative in the Alaska State House of Representatives.

WRIGHT, MURIEL HAZEL (Chocktaw; 1889–), has received numerous awards as an historian, lecturer, editor, and author. A descendant of Allen Wright, former chief of the Choctaw Nation, she was born in 1889, in Lehigh, Indian Territory (now Oklahoma). She began as researcher and writer for the Oklahoma State Historical Society in 1924 and in 1955 became editor of the *Chronicles of Oklahoma*, the society's quarterly magazine. She has authored or co-authored seven books and hundreds of articles.

WYASKET, FRANCIS (Uncompahgre Ute: 1926–   ), past Chairman for the Uintah and Ouray Tribal Business Committee for the Uintah and Ouray Indian Reservation in the State of Utah, was born 1926 in a small community called Ouray, Utah.

Education was received at Ouray and Whiterocks Boarding School and at Alterrra High School in Utah.

A Rancher, he was elected to the Business Committee in 1965 and elected Chairman to that committee which he held for eight years.

Various enterprises were established under his supervision, namely, *Nutuveek* which pertains to hunting of big game for a fee and which gave employment to tribal members as well as income for the tribe. *Bottle Hollow Resort:* the building of this magnificent motel beside a beautiful lake has given employment to tribal members as well as income to the tribe as of today. *Ute Fab Enterprise*: this enterprise builds custom made furniture and fixtures for homes and for Bureau of Indian Affairs Boarding Schools.

❑ ❑ ❑

Wahshungah

Wakechai

Walks in the Water

Ward, Nancy

Washakie

Watie, Stand

Waumegesako (the Wampum)

Wauneka, Annie Dodge

Westerman, Floyd

Whirlwind

White Antelope

White Calf

White Antelope

White Calf

White Antelope

White Calf

White Hair (Pawhuska)

White Man Runs Him

White-Nosed Fox

White Swan

Wild Cat

Winnemucca, Sarah

Wolf Chief

Wolf Plume

Wright, Allen

Wovoka

X

XICOTÉNCATL, DOÑA LUISA (Tlaxcala; fl. 16th century), born Techquilvasin, a beautiful princess of the Tlaxcala kingdom of Mexico, bore on March 22, 1524, the first reported child of mixed European and American Indian blood, Leonor, daughter of the Spanish captain Pedro de Alvarado. Descendants of two sons by this marriage became aligned with the Spanish duchy of Albuquerque.

XICOTÉNCATL THE ELDER (Tlaxcala; fl. 16th century). When the Spanish conquistador Hernando Cortés invaded the Tlaxcala kingdom of Central Mexico in 1519, he first encountered the aged cacique Xicoténcatl the Elder (el viejo), who governed Tizatlán, one of the four districts (*cabaceras*) of the domain. Xicoténcatl was instrumental in allying Tlaxcala with Cortéz against the Aztecs, despite the opposition of his son Xicoténcatl the Younger.

Xicoténcatl the Elder's pre-conquest years were said to have numbered over 120. Son of the nobleman Aztahua, he succeeded Xayamachan as governor of Tizatlán. In 1515 he may have pursued a band of Huexotzincas towards the city of Chalco, though this report probably refers to his son. Xicoténcatl was so old when the Spanish arrived, his wives and daughters had to prop him up and open his eyelids for him to greet the visitors.

After a feeble military resistance to Cortés, Xicoténcatl and the other elders quickly determined that the Spaniards were invincible, perhaps divine. When his son defied him by attacking the Spanish, the old man hastened to placate Cortés, and put the blame on Moctezuma II and the Aztecs. Xicoténcatl and the other chiefs readily complied with Cortés' request for 5,000 Indian auxiliaries in his attack on Montezuma.

Following the momentary setback of the *noche triste* ("sad night") of 1520 in Mexico City, Cortés took refuge in Tlaxcala. Xicoténcatl, taking the Christian name Vicente, accepted baptism, and offered Cortés his daughter Luisa as wife. Cortés passed her on to his captain Pedro Alvarado. Xicoténcatl the Elder may have outlived his son, since the title on his death passed to a nephew, Antonio.

There is some confusion between the two Xicoténcatls, but two critical distinctions remain: the younger was never cacique, and resisted the Spanish to his death. From these differences sprung Cortés' spectacular success in the conquest of Mexico.

XICOTÉNCATL THE YOUNGER (Tlaxcala; fl. 16th century), son of the kingdom's oldest chief attempted to rouse the army against Cortés, despite the opposition of the governing elders, including his father, after the Tlaxcala Indians of Central Mexico chose to make peace with the Spaniard Hernando Cortés following his arrival in 1519. Almost alone, the brave general held the Spaniards in disdain and suspicion, preferring to side with Tlaxcala's traditional enemy the Aztecs.

As his father was quite old at the time of Cortés' arrival, Xicoténcatl was probably in middle age. References to a Xicoténcatl who pursued some Huexotzinca Indians in the vicinity of Chalco in 1515 probably mean the general. He had reached the supreme military post of Tlaxcala, commanding an army estimated at 50,000. Only a fraction of this force was available when the Spanish came, but with his small troop Xicoténcatl attacked Cortés. A fierce, hand-to-hand battle was won by the Spanish. The elders of the kingdom, led by Maxicatzin, cacique of Ocotelolco district, firmly disapproved Xicoténcatl's plans to redouble his attack on the Spanish. He attempted to gain Cortés' confidence, while at the same time forming a desperate plot against him. After abandoning the Spanish camp Xicoténcatl tried to kill Cortés in a sneak attack by night. Failing again, the Indian was forced to flee the kingdom. According to the most likely version of Xicoténcatl the Younger's death, Cortés had him captured and hung at Texcoco, in May of 1521.

The historical confusion of father and son is reflected in another story of Xicoténcatl the Younger's death, that Maxicatzin, in anger, pushed him down some temple steps. There can be no doubt, however, that it was the son who opposed the Spanish to the end, and became a symbol of frustrated patriotism.

XOLOTL (Chichemec; fl. 12th century), in the middle of the 12th century, settled the Valley of Mexico following the destruction of the Toltec empire. With remarkable diplomacy and foresight, Xolotl molded a federation that built many of Central Mexico's most famous cities and gave birth to its most impressive culture, the Aztecs. He was as notable for his descendants as his own achievements.

The Chichimecs were little more than a horde of unrelated barbarian tribes from the north when Xolotl arrived in the valley with his able son Nopaltzin and six powerful vassals. He established himself as the region's high king, dispensing land to Toltec survivors and new arrivals alike, in return for their sworn loyalty. To his regime are attributed the establishments of such important cities as Xochimilco, Chalco, and Texcoco. Xolotl himself erected a garden city called Tenayuco. He placated the natives by marrying Nopaltzin to Azcatlxochitl, niece of the famous Toltec king Topiltzin. 1168, the 47th year of his reign, is given as the date of his most critical diplomatic move. Three princes of the Acolhua race approached with a large army. But Xolotl cooly offered them high positions in his government, and gave two of them his own daughters in marriage. From these alliances sprung several noble houses of Central Mexico.

Placing the government in the hands of his son and sons-in-law, Xolotl retired to his gardens and dedicated himself to beautifying his city. But Nopaltzin had to quash a rebellion led by a Toltec named Nauhyotl. Though an attempt on Xolotl's life failed, he died shortly thereafter. 1232 is usually given as the date, when he was said to have reached the unlikely age of 180, after a reign of 112 years.

However fantastic the legends surrounding Xolotl, his legacy cannot be denied. Counted among his illustrious descendants are Acamapichtli, the first Aztec king, and Nezahuallpilli, last ruler of the Tlaxcala city of Texcoco.

Y

YAHAHAJO (Seminole; fl. 19th century), was a Seminole chief. His name meant Mad Wolf. He held the title of second principal war chief during the wars resisting removal and was considered the most skilled hunter in the nation. One of a contingent selected to inspect the western lands designated for Seminole settlement, he found the lands suitable and signed an agreement ratifying the treaty of Payne's Landing. That treaty concluded in 1832 agreed to Seminole removal. The agreement was looked upon by the Seminole as a fraud and disregarded by them.

When the Seminoles resumed their hostilities against the U.S. he joined the anti-American forces of Mikanopy. He was killed in battle.

YANEGUA (Cherokee; fl. 19th century), Big Bear was an Eastern Cherokee chief. He was prominent during his life, but is remembered by few Cherokees today. He was a signer of two treaties in 1798 and 1805 by which the Cherokees gave away large tracts of their land to the U.S.

As consideration for his signature on another land treaty with the U.S. in 1819, he was given 640 acres within the ceded territory.

YAN MAOW (Bannock) or *Big Nose*, born in 1830 was a signer of the Fort Brigger Treaty in 1868.

YARRINCE, CARLOS ANTONIO (Yarrinces; fl. 18th century), or Larrince was a notorious brigand who during the 1760s both menaced and aided the Spanish in their efforts to colonize Nicaragua. He was chief of an Indian tribe called the Yarrinces, who were considered members of the Carib Indian family. Though his people regarded themselves the shock troops of the Sambo Indian kings, Carlos Antonio was an opportunist, serving whoever promised to serve him best in return.

Carlos Antonio was born before 1750, and as a young man had been converted to Christianity by missionaries on the Nicaraguan frontier (the eastern, or inland, shores of Lake Nicaragua). His people made their home in the modern department of Boaco. In 1762 Carlos Antonio emerged as a thorn in the Spanish side when he led an attack on their settlements in Chontales, apparently in alliance with Mosquito Indians from the Atlantic coast. The series of attacks was probably planned by the British.

By 1768, however, Yarrince and his Indian brothers had switched their alliance to Spain. Chief Carlos offered his support and 500 warriors to Domingo Cabello, Spanish governor in León department, in return for the title of "captain and governor of the Caribs." The next year, Yarrince kept his bargain by capturing and delivering the Carib marauder Pangil, who in 1767 had sacked the Spanish settlement at Camoapa.

Carlos Antonio Yarrince is often confused with his tribesman Carlos Matías Yarrince, whose emergence as chief by 1779 suggest that the old chief had by that time died. The pattern of readily changed loyalties by the Yarrinces continued, however, as the Indians were soon taking the English side in the battle for Nicaragua.

YELLOW FLOWER (Ute) called *Joan*, died in 1873.

YELLOW ROBE, DR. EVELYN (Dakota; 20th century), an internationally known speech pathologist, is a Dakota-Brule Sioux who was born in Rapid City, South Dakota, the daughter of the educator Chauncey Yellow Robe. She graduated from Mt. Holyoke College and in 1944 began teaching, first at Mt. Holyoke and then at Vassar College. Part of her research work included the recording of the Dakota language. In 1946 the Indian Council Fire awarded her the Indian Achievement Medal.

She received her Ph.D. from the Northwestern University School of Speech in 1954 and traveled to Paris on a Fulbright Scholarship to study the physiology of the layrnx. When she returned to the United States, she was a lecturer at Northwestern. Since her marriage in 1959 to Dr. Hans Finkbeiner, she has lived in Germany.

YELLOW THUNDER (Winnebago; 1774–1874), properly Wakunchakookah, a Winnebago chief born 1774, was a respected tribal counselor. The Winnebago tribes had always occupied lands surrounding Lake Winnebago and Green Bay, Wisconsin, but the U.S. government was determined to remove them to a reservation in northeastern Iowa and southeastern Minnesota. In 1837 Yellow Thunder and other chiefs travelled to Washington D.C. to consult with President Andrew Jackson, who refused to speak with them. Duped into signing a treaty (Nov. 1) ceding all Winnebago lands east of the Mississippi River to the U.S., the delegation understood that the tribes would have eight years in which to relocate. The U.S. government soon informed them that the treaty actually allowed eight months only. Yellow Thunder advised resistance, but in 1840 troops were sent to Portage, Wisconsin to begin removal forceably. Upon false rumor that he was planning revolt, Yellow Thunder was placed in chains, but soon released. Because the chiefs decided that any further resistance would be futile, the removal was accomplished peacefully. In 1841 Yellow Thunder abandoned his tribe and returned to Wisconsin with his wife and on 40 acres of land about eight miles north of Portage established a homestead where he died February, 1874.

YELTATZIE (Haida).

YENAHTSETL (Tlingit) was a chief in the 1880s.

YESNO, JOHNNY (Ojibwa; November 8, 1938–   ), an Ojibwa producer, broadcaster, and actor for radio, television and film, was born on Fort Hope Reserve in Northeast Ontario Canada. He attended the University of Waterloo and worked as a surveyor and engineering technician. After winning a national championship for Indian dancing, he was given the role of an Indian in a television series and won the "Wilderness Award" for his outstanding performance. His acting career also included a part in Walt Disney's *Biography of a Grizzly*. In 1964 he started a weekly radio program, *Indian Magazine*, for the Canadian Broadcasting Corporation. As host and co-producer he tried to make the show a forum for the exchange of Indian opinions and for the presentation of Indian viewpoints to non-Indians. Active in Canadian Indian affairs, he served on the executive board of the Canadian Indian Centre of Toronto. His unusual name comes from the response of one of his ancestors during treaty negotiations. Offered all the land he wanted in exchange for the mineral rights, the ancestor nodded *yes* to the first half of the bargain and *no* to the second.

YOHOLO, CHITTEE (Seminole; fl. 19th century), was a Seminole war chief. He led a successful night attack against U.S. and Creek forces on March 28-29, 1836. He captured so many scalps that he was known to his people as the *Snake that makes noise.*

He was a great terrorist and guerilla fighter. One of his tactics was to steal the beef cattle grazing near an army garrison and allow the soldiers to starve.

He eventually gave himself to the U.S. authorities at St. Augustine and was removed to Indian territory.

YOHOLOMICCO (Creek; fl. late 18th and early 19th centuries), was a Creek chief who was well known in the late 18th and early 19th centuries. As chief of Eufalo, a strategic town, he wielded considerable power. He was an ally of the pro-American chief, William MacIntosh. Respected as a great speaker he was compared favorably to the great Creek orator of the upper towns, Opothleyeholo. Unfortunately, in his orations he spoke glowingly of the plans of the U.S. for improving the lot of the Creek people. this disgusted the Creek people who had strong anti-American sentiments. Eventually he was deposed as chief of Eufalo town.

In 1826, before his downfall, he went to Washington as a member of a delegation to discuss cession of lands to the U.S. He eventually agreed to move to Arkansas, but died during the migration. He is remembered as a strong proponent of education for Indians.

YONAGUSKA (Cherokee; 1759–1839), was the most prominent of all the eastern Cherokee chiefs. His name was translated as Drowning Bear. While others accommodated the U.S. government by migrating to Indian territory, Yonaguska and his followers steadfastly refused to leave, moving further into the hills. A great orator, he is primarily remembered as a quasi religious leader who had a great moral influence on his people.

He and his followers eventually settled near Succo Creek on land purchased for them by Col. William Thomas, Yonaguska's adopted son. It was there as an old man of 60 that he became seriously ill. The illness culminated in a trance during which he was taken for dead. After 24 hours, however, he awoke to report that he had spoken with God who had given him a message for all Cherokees. He stopped drinking, exhorting his followers to do the same. He organized his eastern band into a temperance society and had each member of the great council sign a pledge not to drink whiskey. From that time until Yonaguska's death, drunkenness was unknown among the eastern Cherokees.

Throughout his life he was suspicious of whites and rebuffed all of the government's efforts to persuade his band to move west. He was especially skeptical of missionaries and the Christian religions. When presented with a copy of the Book of Matthew he was quoted as saying, "It seems to be a good book—strange that the white people are not better, after having had it so long." He died at nearly the age of 80 in April, 1839. The Cherokee removal which he had fought so long began in 1838.

He was an anomaly in Cherokee society famed for its success in accommodating itself to white culture.

YORK, EMMETT (Chocktaw; 1903–July 26, 1971), served as chief of the Misissippi Band of Choctaw Indians from 1965 until his death at the age of 68. In March, 1971, he had begun a term as president of the Southeastern Tribes after a 22-year membership on the Choctaw Tribal Council. Just before his death, the Bureau of Indian Affairs honored him with an award for his outstanding contribution. He is buried at Pearl River (Mississippi) Reservation.

YOUNG MAN AFRAID OF HIS HORSE (Dakota; fl. 19th century), was an Oglala Sioux chief who, although he opposed incursion of the white man into his people's country, nevertheless led his close followers in averting the massacre of a seven-man commission sent to negotiate for the purchase of the Black Hills, September 17, 1875.

A contemporary of Red Cloud, Young Man Afraid of His Horse's Indian name, Tasunkakokipapi, has been misinterpreted by white men. It really means "They fear even his horses," or that the young man was so brave that just the sight of his horses frightened his enemies. He was prominent in the Platte Bridge fight of 1865.

YOUPEE, WILLIAM (Dakota; 20th century), now executive director of the National Tribal Chairman's Association (NTCA), was the founder of this organization and its first president. Previously, he

served 18 years on the tribal council of the Fort Peck
Assiniboine and Sioux tribes reservation at Popular, Montana, including ten years as chairman of
the Tribal Executive Board. His other activities include former membership on the Indian Labor Advisory Board and National Indian Chairmen
Association and present membership on the board
of the Miss American Indian Pageant. He is a vocal
defender of strengthened tribal government.

Yahahajo

Yan Maow

Yellow Flower

Yellow Robe, Evelyn

Yellow Thunder

Yeltatzie, Lucinda

Yenahtsetl

Yoholo, Chittee

Yoholomicco

Z

ZUNI, JOSE A. (Isleta Pueblo; April 26, 1921–   ), a public administrator, is an Isleta Pueblo born in Isleta Pueblo, New Mexico. He served with the U.S. Army Air Force in World War II and has been active in the affairs of the Isleta Pueblo community, as lieutenant governor, tribal judge, and a member of the Isleta Tribal Council. Now in Stewart, Nevada, he is superintendent of the Nevada agency of the Bureau of Indian Affairs.

ZUNIGHA, WAYNE (Zuñi-Delaware; Sept. 28, 1931–   ), is a regional and city planner. Born in Claremore, Oklahoma, he received his bachelor's and master's degrees from Oklahoma State University. He served as director of planning for the states of Kentucky and West Virginia and in the mid-1970s was executive director of the Cherokee Tribal Planning Board for the Eastern Bank of Cherokee. He also assisted in the coordination of the economic, social, and physical development of the Cherokee Reservation in North Carolina.

□ □ □